All-in-One
Guitar
JAM TRACKS

ROCK ★ BLUES ★ JAZZ ★ COUNTRY ★ METAL ★ FUNK

AUDIO ACC

MW00559462

by CHRIS AMELAR

To access audio visit:
www.halleonard.com/mylibrary

1859-3892-5513-8323

ISBN 978-1-4803-6039-6

HAL•LEONARD® CORPORATION
7777 W. BLUEMOUND RD. P.O. BOX 13819 MILWAUKEE, WI 53213

Visit Hal Leonard Online at
www.halleonard.com

5   How to Use This Book

7   CHAPTER 1: BLUES JAMS

7   Introduction to Blues Guitar

8   Skipping Around

11   Pinto

13   Dirty Old Man

15   King of the Bend

19   T-Bone Steak

22   The Bayou

24   Cold Cruel World

26   John Q. Public

28   True Blue

30   Road Runner

33   CHAPTER 2: COUNTRY JAMS

33   Introduction to Country Guitar

34   Cowpoke

37   Tennessee Strut

39   Whiskey 'n' Diesel

42   Barn Burner

45   Southern Belle

48   Promenade

50   Homestead

52   Western Sunset

54   Ropin' and Ridin'

57   Honky Tonk Shuffle

59   CHAPTER 3: FUNK JAMS

59   Introduction to Funk Guitar

60   Back to the Bay

62   Flip Flop

65   Marachino

68   Metric

71   Fried Eggs

73   Antimatter

76   Rebound

78   Suburban Jungle

80   Late Nite

83   Makeover

86 CHAPTER 4: JAZZ JAMS

86 Introduction to Jazz Guitar

87 You Are All the Things

90 Blooze in Eff

93 My Prints Will Come Someday

96 Dolphins on Green St.

99 Impersonations

101 Bobby and Sal

104 Confiscation

107 Stellar

110 Record Me

112 I've Got Changes

115 CHAPTER 5: METAL JAMS

115 Introduction to Metal Guitar

116 Raceway Park

119 Shock Treatment

121 Saddle Up

123 Forward March

125 Polka Time

128 Shakin' the Boot

130 Shufflin'

133 Hellboys from Cow

136 Oddly Enough

139 Underworld

142 CHAPTER 6: ROCK JAMS

142 Introduction to Rock Guitar

143 Rolling Crows

146 Young Agnes

149 Hot and Cold

152 Nervosa

155 Daisy

159 Good Company

162 All Hail Sammy

165 Crawling Along

168 Slash and Burn

171 Odds and Ends

174 Guitar Notation Legend

How to Use This Book

In order for you to obtain maximum value from this package, it's important for you to read the description of each tune first before trying to improvise. Many of the tracks contain key changes and other things that may throw you off if you are not aware of them. It's also essential for you to learn and memorize the scale fingerings for each tune so you can improvise smoothly without having to guess which notes go with which chord.

For each exercise, you are provided with three sample phrases that will give you ideas and expand your soloing vocabulary. These phrases vary in difficulty from easy to moderately tricky to advanced. Be sure to look at the standard notation for each lick to get any helpful left hand fingerings.

Try recording your jams: this will allow you to hear yourself the way others hear you. If you really want to have fun, invite a friend over and jam together, trading licks back and forth.

CHAPTER 1: BLUES JAMS

INTRODUCTION TO BLUES GUITAR

The blues has been a favorite style of guitarists for over a hundred years. This timeless music has influenced practically every other form of music that exists. Certainly one of the best ways to learn how to improvise is by playing the blues. Its simple chords and cyclical (repeating) form create an endlessly satisfying framework over which you can explore and develop new musical ideas. Always the same yet forever challenging, the blues is, for most musicians, the first style which teaches them how to improvise or create music on the spot. Like any style, the blues can take on many forms. With this in mind I've created ten unique and highly diverse blues rhythm tracks that will help you develop and improve your improvisational skills and knowledge of soloing. They will also help you to gain greater insight into the many nuances and stylistic elements of this genre. This, in turn, will give you more confidence in live-playing situations. I have built into each track the kind of interaction, dynamics, and occasional breaks that would occur naturally if you were playing with a real group. Most of all, these tracks were designed to provide you with many hours of fun and enjoyment as you learn the skills and techniques needed to become a great blues guitarist.

SKIPPING AROUND

"Skipping Around" is best described as a Texas shuffle. This feel was made popular by the late, great Stevie Ray Vaughan in such songs as "Pride and Joy" and "Empty Arms." It's a simple twelve-bar blues in E with a turnaround at the end of every chorus. Although the turnaround contains complex chords such as Gdim7 and F#m7♭5, it isn't necessary for you to address them in your improvising. They are passing chords and will not clash with the scales given in Figs. 1-5.

Fig. 1 E minor blues and Fig. 5 E minor pentatonic are the best scale choices to use against the entire progression. Fig. 1 specifically is a lot of fun because there are so many stock blues licks contained within its fingering. Try playing Fig. 1 with hammer-ons and pull-offs rather than picking each note. This will give your phrasing a more traditional sound. Also a light bend on the high G (3rd fret, 1st string) adds a nice touch. For a slightly jazzier sound try the three Mixolydian scales in Figs. 2-4. Each scale works only against a corresponding dominant chord with the same root. For example: E Mixolydian can only be used over E, E7 or E9, just as A Mixolydian should only be used over A or A7.

The time signature of 12/8 is most often used in writing a shuffle. One element that gives a Texas shuffle its characteristic skipping feel is the accent on every third eighth note. For a really interesting effect try playing on just the even numbered eighth notes (*i.e.*, 2, 4, 6, 8, 10, 12). This creates a *polyrhythm* which will build tension and excitement in your phrases.

Another rhythmic technique used by blues players is to *rake* into your notes. Raking means to strum quickly across the strings—with either an upstroke or downstroke—stopping on the note that you want to sound. All of the strings must be muted with your left hand except for the last string in the rake. Also, look at the sample licks in Figs. 6, 7 and 8 for more ideas.

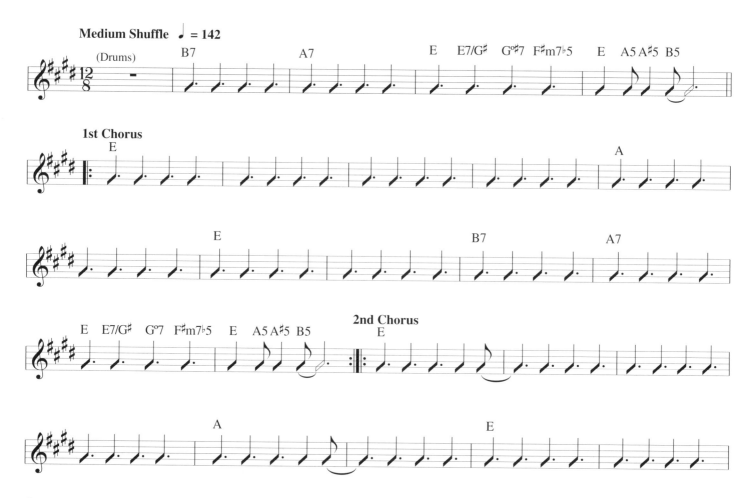

Scales for "Skipping Around"

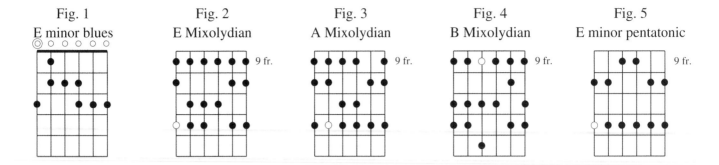

Fig. 1
E minor blues

Fig. 2
E Mixolydian

Fig. 3
A Mixolydian

Fig. 4
B Mixolydian

Fig. 5
E minor pentatonic

Sample Licks for "Skipping Around"

Fig. 6

Fig. 7

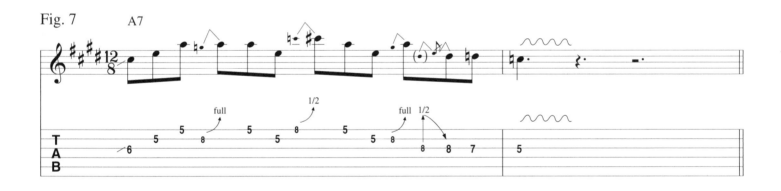

Fig. 8

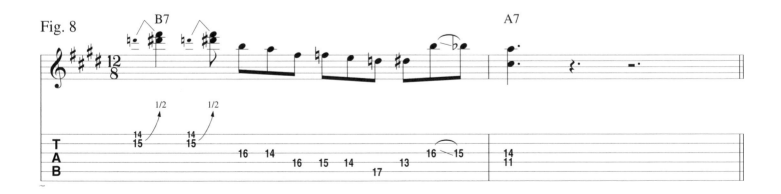

PINTO

"Pinto" is a funky twenty-four bar blues in C that has essentially the same form as a regular twelve bar blues except that each chord lasts twice as long. There is also a break that occurs in the 19th and 20th measures of every chorus. This break does not mean that you should stop playing. In fact this recurring break allows you, the improviser, to take the spotlight and show off your meanest licks *a capella*.

For this tune you are given five scale choices. The first two (Figs. 1 and 2) are the same scale, C minor blues, played at two different areas of the fretboard. As in the previous exercise, both Figs. 1 and 2 work equally well over the entire progression whereas Figs. 3, 4 and 5 have more specific applications. Fig. 3, C Mixolydian, sounds well over C9, C7, and B♭/C, Fig. 4, F dominant pentatonic, works over F9 and during the break at measure 19, and G dominant pentatonic works against the G9 and G7♯5 chords.

The sample licks in Figs. 6, 7 and 8 each work over a different chord in the progression. Fig. 6 is a well-known lick heard on countless blues recordings. Although it is written as a C9 lick, it will sound great anytime during the progression. Fig. 7 demonstrates the technique of *targeting*. Targeting is when you play several non-harmonic tones and resolve them to a nearby chord tone. In Fig. 7 the last note, A (a chord tone in F9), is directly preceeded by the notes C♭, B♭, and A♭ (non-chord tones). This is a good example of tension and release. Fig. 8 is the most difficult lick. It contains a variety of techniques and is specifically written to work only over the 17th and 18th measures (G9 to F9).

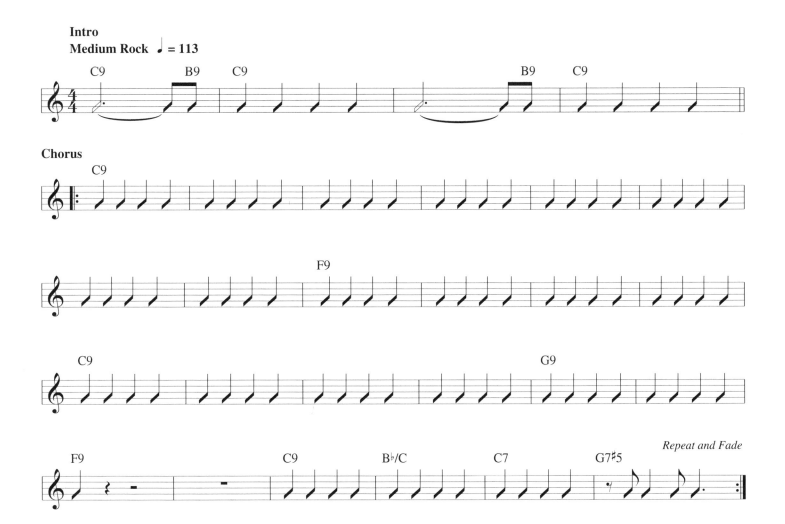

Scales for "Pinto"

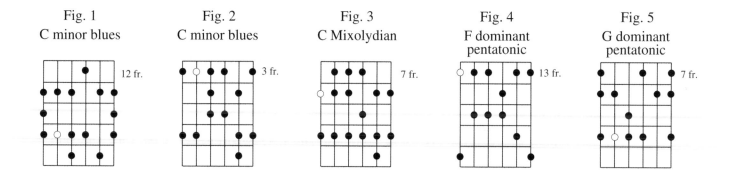

Fig. 1
C minor blues

Fig. 2
C minor blues

Fig. 3
C Mixolydian

Fig. 4
F dominant
pentatonic

Fig. 5
G dominant
pentatonic

Sample Licks for "Pinto"

Fig. 6

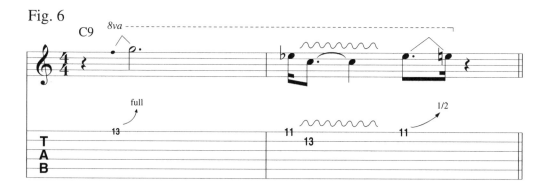

Fig. 7

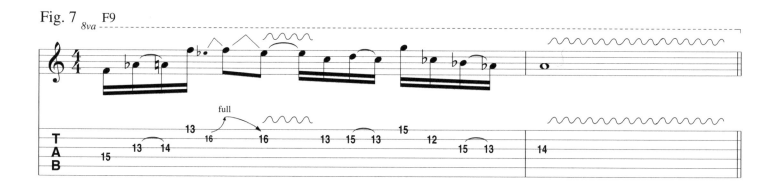

Fig. 8

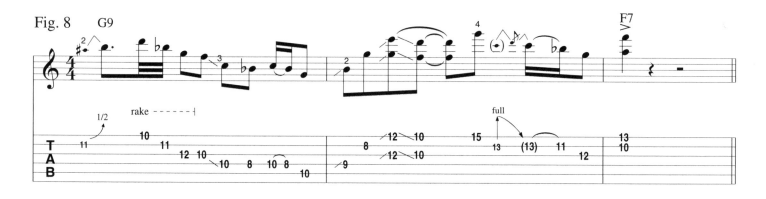

DIRTY OLD MAN

"Dirty Old Man," begins with the last four measures of the progression on E♭9. This chord represents the fundamental difference between this progression and more standard blues progressions. Normally in a G blues you would find D7 (V chord) moving to a C7 (IV chord) during the ninth and tenth measures, but in this case we have E♭9 (♭VI dominant chord) moving to C/D (V chord substitute). In order to improvise smoothly over this section try using the E♭ Mixolydian scale (Fig. 3) for the E♭9 chord, and either the G minor or G major blues scales (Figs. 1 and 2) for the C/D chord. The C major blues scale in Fig. 4 is an optional scale for playing on the C7 chord only.

The sample licks in Figs. 5-7 are designed to work over specific chords in the progression. Fig. 5 should be played against G7 exclusively. In Fig. 5 make sure that you hold the first bent note while picking the second. Fig. 6 demonstrates the use of passing tones over C7 in a blues context. It begins with a double bend which is done by bending the F on the 3rd string with your 3rd finger (with your 2nd and 1st fingers on the 9th and 8th frets respectively) and bending the A on the 2nd string with your pinky alone. The third lick, Fig. 7, works over the E♭9 chord moving to C/D. It contains *double stops* which means you play two notes (simultaneously) with one finger.

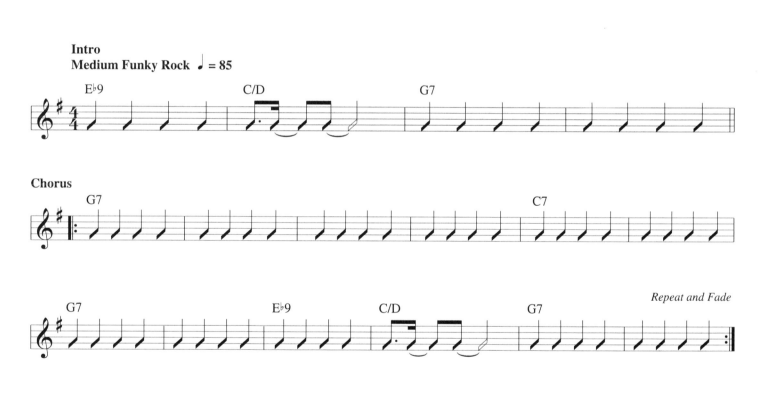

Scales for "Dirty Old Man"

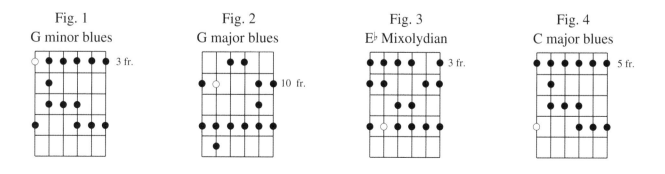

| Fig. 1 | Fig. 2 | Fig. 3 | Fig. 4 |
| G minor blues | G major blues | E♭ Mixolydian | C major blues |

Sample Licks for "Dirty Old Man"

Fig. 5

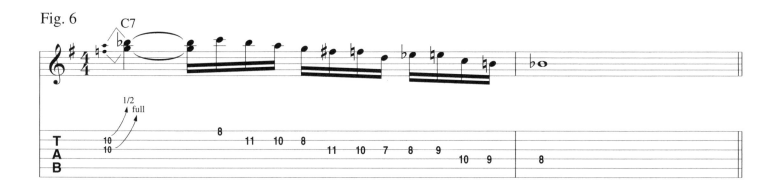

Fig. 6

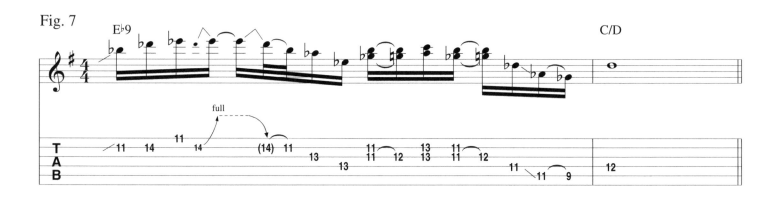

Fig. 7

KING OF THE BEND

This tune's title and chord progression were inspired by a great guitarist and close friend of mine, Harry Jacobson. "King of the Road" is actually built around two twelve-bar progressions. The first is a standard blues progression while the second is the same as the first except for the last four bars. In bar nine of the second progression instead of going to the V chord it goes to a III dominant and then a IV dominant in the following measure. The last chord of the second progression sets up a modulation to a new key. Each pair of progressions modulates up a half step (one fret) the first two times and then up a fourth (five frets) the last time. In other words, you will solo in A for twenty-four bars, then B♭ for the next twenty-four bars, then B for the next twenty-four bars and finally E for the last twelve bars.

The suggested scales for this exercise only apply to the *first* pair of choruses, (or the first twenty-four bars.) After that you must *transpose* them to the next appropriate key. For instance when you reach the twenty-fifth measure, move the A minor pentatonic fingering (Fig. 1) up one fret to B♭. This must be done for all the scales as you get to each new key.

Figs. 1 and 2 should be used over the I7 chord in each key, Fig. 3 is a good choice for the IV7 chord, and Fig. 4 sounds right against the V7 chord. Fig. 5 should be used only over the III7 chord of each key and nothing else.

The sample licks in Figs. 6-8 work over the I7 chord of each of the first three keys respectively. If you're in doubt, match the chord symbols over each lick with the chords in the progression. Fig. 6 contains a "reverse bend" which means you must bend the string before picking it and then release. In Fig. 7 you must "trill" on the last note. In this case it means to hammer-on and pull-off quickly between the sixth and seventh frets of the third string.

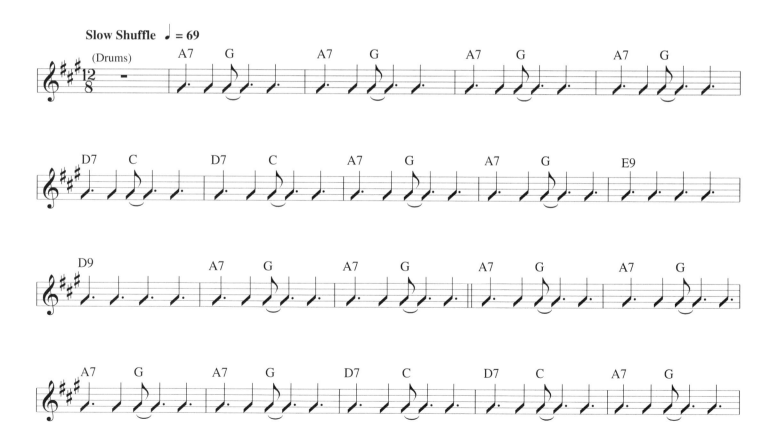

King of the Bend

Scales for "King of the Bend"

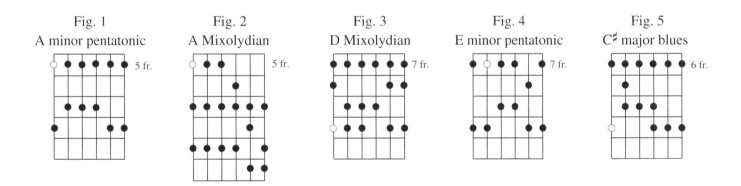

Fig. 1
A minor pentatonic

Fig. 2
A Mixolydian

Fig. 3
D Mixolydian

Fig. 4
E minor pentatonic

Fig. 5
C# major blues

Sample Licks for "King of the Bend"

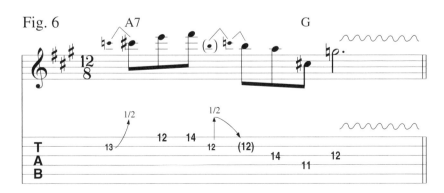

Fig. 6

Fig. 7

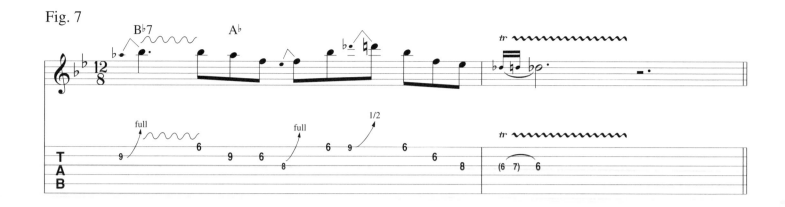

Fig. 8

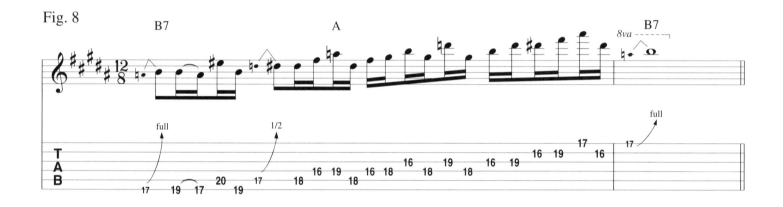

King of the Bend

T-BONE STEAK

"T-Bone Steak," is a fast swing blues in B♭. Much of the arrangement is punctuated by various horn figures. Like the second track there are stylistic breaks at the beginning of several of the choruses which allow you to solo alone. Harmonically, this is a simple exercise. The only place where the chords become more involved is during the last chorus. However if you look closely you'll see that the chords which have been added are simply chromatic approach chords a half step below the main chords. Since they only last for a short period of time it isn't necessary for you to address them in your solo with a scale change.

The first scale (Fig. 1) is actually the B♭ minor blues scale with two passing tones (C and G) added in the upper register. These passing tones are commonly used with this fingering. Try playing the scale with and without them to hear the difference. The sample lick in Fig. 7 demonstrates how they might be used in context. Another example of passing tones is in Fig. 6. Here the passing tones are mostly chromatic. It's also interesting to observe that almost every note in the chromatic scale is contained within Fig. 6. This proves that you can play almost any note over any chord if you do it the right way! The other scales (Figs. 2-4) should be used only against dominant chords with the same root, respectively Fig. 2 with B♭7, Fig. 3 with E♭7 and Fig. 4 with F7.

Although this tune is written in 4/4 time the eighth notes are not played evenly. Instead you should play your eighth notes with a swing feel. To do this, play the eighth note as if you are playing only the first and third beats of a triplet. Try playing the second sample phrase (Fig. 6) this way.

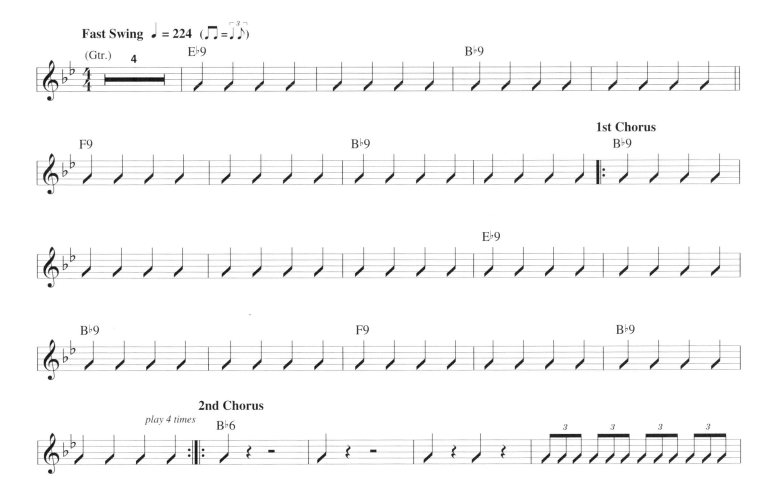

Scales for "T-Bone Steak"

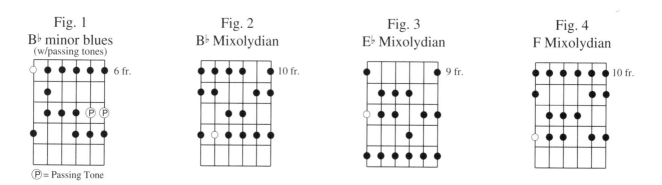

Fig. 1
Bb minor blues
(w/passing tones)
6 fr.
P = Passing Tone

Fig. 2
Bb Mixolydian
10 fr.

Fig. 3
Eb Mixolydian
9 fr.

Fig. 4
F Mixolydian
10 fr.

Sample Licks for "T-Bone Steak"

Fig. 5

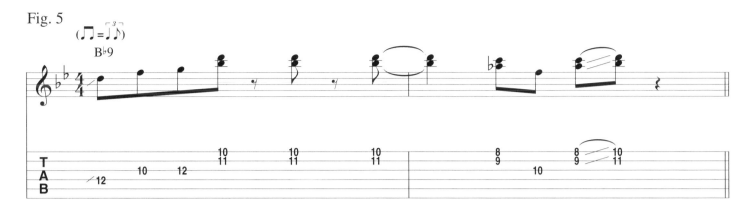

Fig. 6

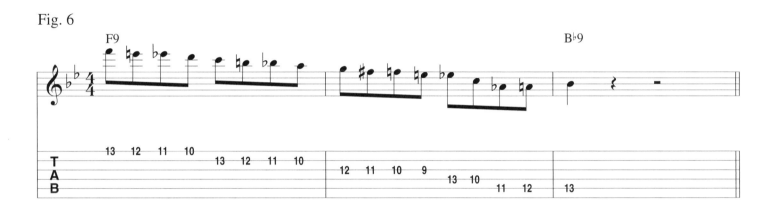

Fig. 7

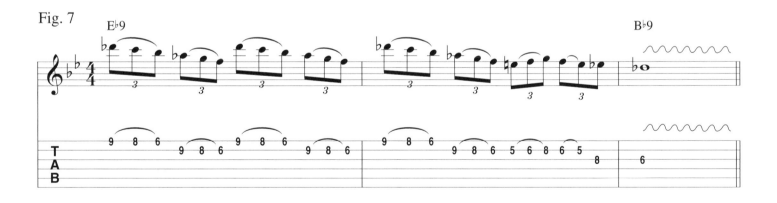

THE BAYOU

Harmonically, "The Bayou" is a departure from the other tunes. Instead of having mostly dominant chords, this track primarily contains minor chords making it a *minor blues*. There are also several altered chords requiring scales different from the ones we've had so far.

The first scale in Fig. 1, D minor pentatonic, can be used over the entire exercise. Also Fig. 4, D Aeolian, can be used over every chord except Bb7b5. For that chord try using Fig. 5, Bb Mixolydian #4 (sometimes called Lydian Dominant). This scale is the same as regular Bb Mixolydian but its fourth note is one half step higher. Figs. 2 and 3 are optional. You may use Fig. 2, E Locrian, against the Em7b5 chord and Fig. 3, A Super Locrian over A7#5.

Changing scales in midstream is one of the hardest things to do while improvising. This is also one of the most sought after skills by beginning improvisers. In order to change scales smoothly, you must first be completely comfortable with the scales you are using and be absolutely certain *where* in the music the changes take place. This is important because in order to switch scales smoothly you must be able to *anticipate* the change before it happens.

This allows you time to mentally prepare yourself for the new fingering. Always remember that it's the *last* note you play which justifies your phrase. In other words, if you end on a "good" note everyone will think what came before that note was intentional (even if it wasn't). But if you end on a "sour" note they will usually ignore what came before it (no matter how cool it was) and remember that you flubbed your solo!! (And if there are any guitar players in the audience, forget it!)

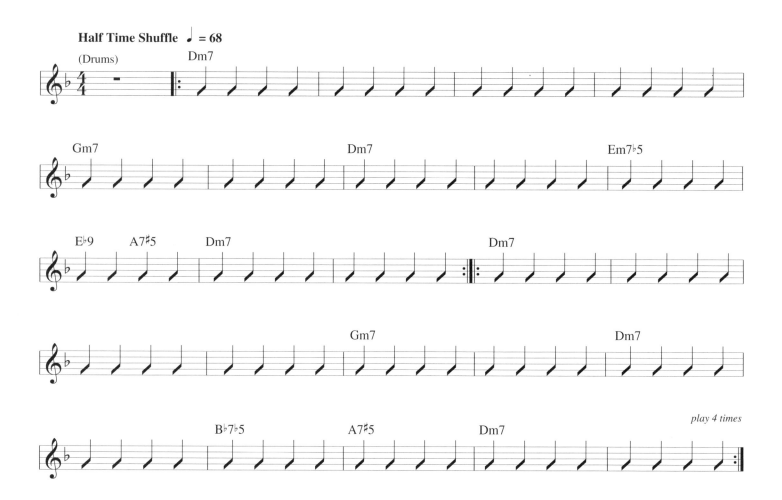

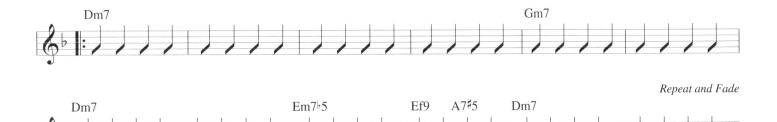

Repeat and Fade

Scales for "The Bayou"

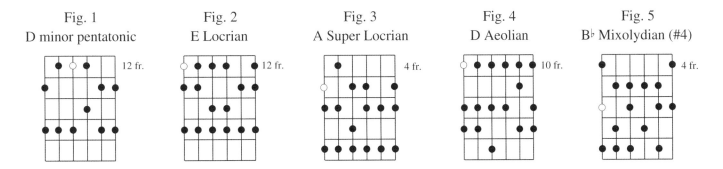

Fig. 1	Fig. 2	Fig. 3	Fig. 4	Fig. 5
D minor pentatonic	E Locrian	A Super Locrian	D Aeolian	B♭ Mixolydian (#4)

Sample Licks for "The Bayou"

Fig. 6

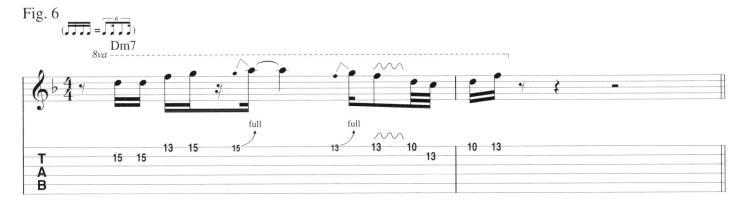

Fig. 7

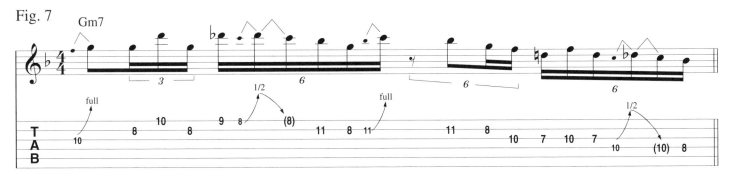

Fig. 8

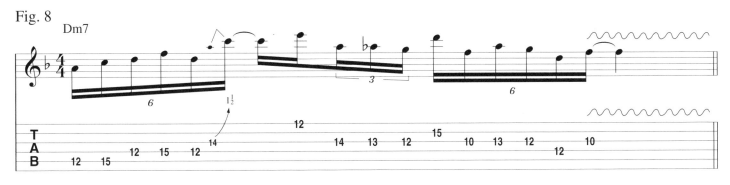

COLD CRUEL WORLD

"Cold Cruel World" is a minor blues. There are only three chords in the entire tune and they are all minor (Fm7, B♭m7 and Cm7). This predominance of minor chords enhances the tune's dark, lamenting mood. Since all three chords are diatonically related to the key of A♭ major (F minor), you can use any scale or mode related to this key (*i.e.*, B♭ Dorian, C Phrygian, D♭ Lydian, etc...)

If we look at the first sample scale, Fig. 1, we see that it's an F minor pentatonic scale with the note G added to the fingering. This scale is actually the same as an F natural minor scale without the D♭. Because it's missing this one note it can be used in an F Dorian or F Aeolian context. Figs. 1, 2 and 4 all work over the entire exercise whereas Fig. 3 should only be used with the Cm7 chord.

As a stylistic suggestion, try using long sustaining notes and mournful bends to emphasize the inherently sad quality of this track. It's also valuable to practice developing your solo from a low dynamic point to a high one over a specific amount of time. Since this tune is only six choruses long you can work on building your ideas up from simple to complex phrases.

The first two sample licks (Figs. 5 and 6) emphasize the use of bending in a blues context. Fig. 5 begins with a bend that you must hold up while playing other notes. This is followed by two reverse bends to be played with your first finger. In Fig. 6 you're required to pull off your third finger to your first, simultaneously bending up a whole step with your first finger. You must also slide into a bend on the last note. To do this properly bend the string a little as you are sliding.

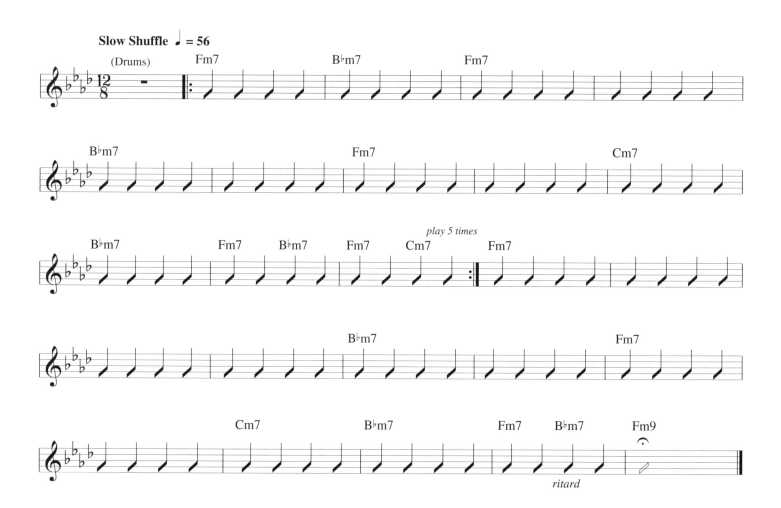

Scales for "Cold Cruel World"

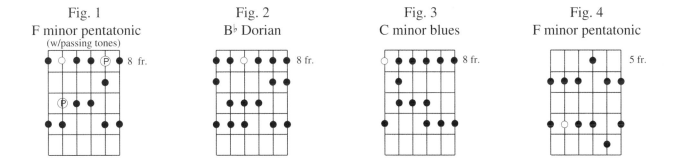

Fig. 1
F minor pentatonic
(w/passing tones)
8 fr.

Fig. 2
B♭ Dorian
8 fr.

Fig. 3
C minor blues
8 fr.

Fig. 4
F minor pentatonic
5 fr.

Sample Licks for "Cold Cruel World"

Fig. 5

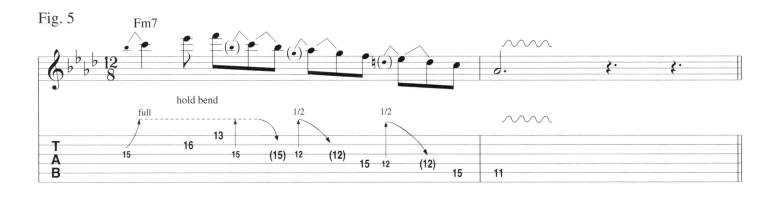

Fig. 6

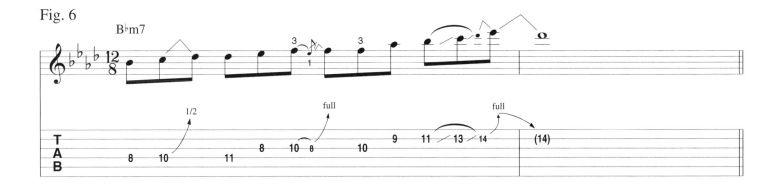

Fig. 7

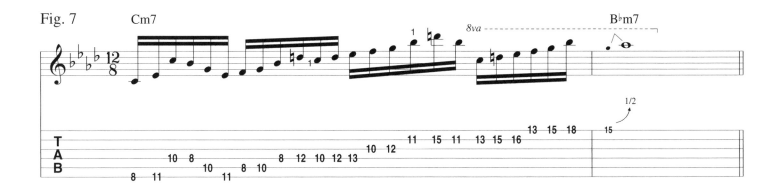

JOHN Q. PUBLIC

"John Q. Public" is a straight ahead, driving rock blues in B major. Chordally, it's very simple. The recurring turnaround at the end of each chorus does not significantly add any harmonic challanges. As a soloist you can ignore the bass notes in the slash chords and simply improvise off of the upper chord symbols. Also note that the A5 and A♯5 chords are *approach* and *passing* chords. It is, therefore, not necessary for you to address them in a specific way in your solo.

The scales include Fig. 1 B minor pentatonic and Fig. 4 B minor blues. Both of these scales work well over the whole tune. Fig. 2, E Dominant Pentatonic, is an optional scale choice for the E5 chords only and Fig. 3, F♯ Mixolydian, is just for F♯5. I have purposely written many of the scale fingerings for each track in the same position on the fretboard. This will allow you to switch between them easily without having to move your hand. This is also the reason why many of the scale fingerings in this book do not start on their roots.

Although the first sample phrase (Fig. 5) is written to work over B5, it can be used anywhere in this exercise. Make sure that you slide into the bend so that it sounds like one large bend rather than two separate actions. Unlike Fig. 5, Fig. 6 should only be used over the first two measures (B5 to E5). Also make sure that you start this lick on your second finger. The first two notes should be very short. The last lick (Fig.7) has been written to work specifically over F♯5 moving to E5. Be aware that the last two notes should ring together.

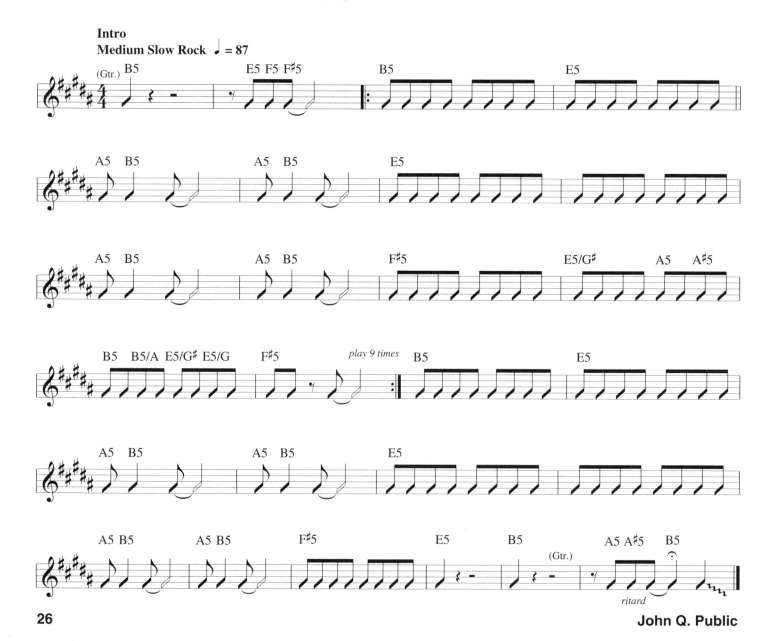

Scales for "John Q. Public"

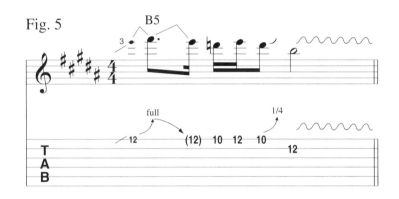

Fig. 1	Fig. 2	Fig. 3	Fig. 4
B minor pentatonic	E dominant pentatonic	F♯ Mixolydian	B minor blues

Sample Licks for "John Q. Public"

Fig. 5

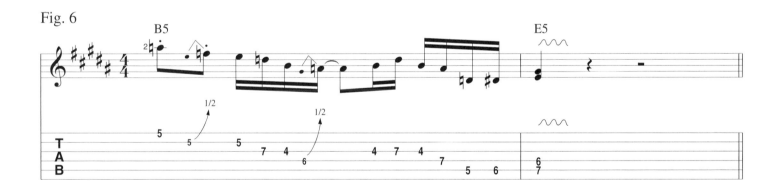

Fig. 6

Fig. 7

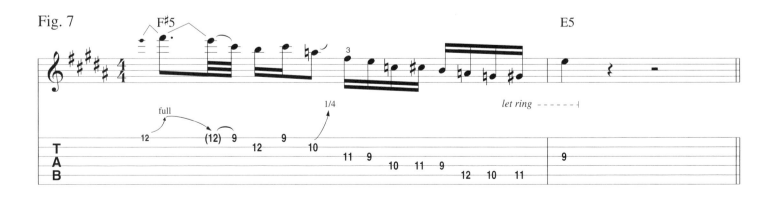

TRUE BLUE

"True Blue" is the only track so far that does not follow the normal twelve-bar format. Instead it is sixteen bars long. It is identical to a regular blues in E except that two extra measures of E7 are added in bars ten and eleven. The recurring turnaround in bars fifteen and sixteen is also the same as it would be in a normal blues.

Non-twelve bar forms are played fairly often in the blues especially by older artists such as Muddy Waters or Freddie King. Often they are the result of an extended vocal phrase or recurring lick that's heard throughout the song.

The scale choices for this track include the E major blues (Fig. 1) and the E minor blues (Fig. 2). Note: they have the same fingering except one starts in open position and the other in ninth position. Both scales work over the whole exercise but Fig. 2 may sound a little more "stylistically correct" especially if you incorporate bends and slurs (hammer-ons, pull-offs and slides). Fig. 3 is actually an A9 arpeggio (A, C♯, E, G, B) which works perfectly against the A7 chord. And finally B dominant pentatonic (Fig. 4) which is an alternate choice over the B7 chords.

The last sample lick, Fig. 7, is an excellent example of how to use chromaticism in the blues. It's written to work over the eleventh and twelfth measures of the chorus, B7 going to E. Notice how every note in the chromatic scale with the exception of C is used over the B7 chord. This demonstrates an important concept which is that any note can work as long as its placed within the proper context. The proper context is usually determined by a number of factors including the style of the music, where the chord progression is going, and how it's resolving. All these things contribute to the overall degree of tension and release.

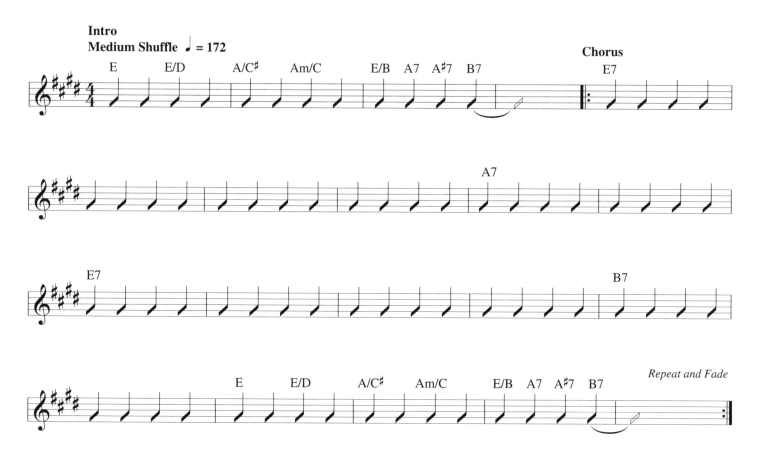

Scales for "True Blue"

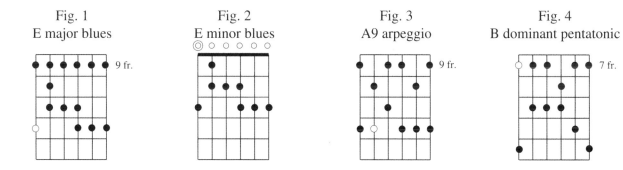

Fig. 1
E major blues

Fig. 2
E minor blues

Fig. 3
A9 arpeggio

Fig. 4
B dominant pentatonic

Sample Licks for "True Blue"

Fig. 6

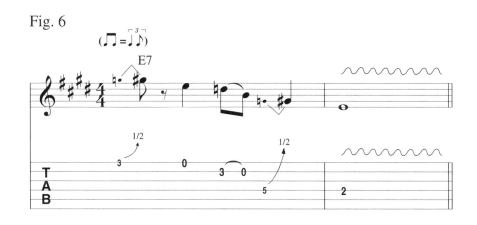

Fig. 6

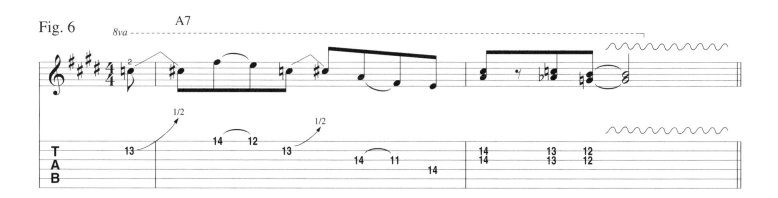

Fig. 7

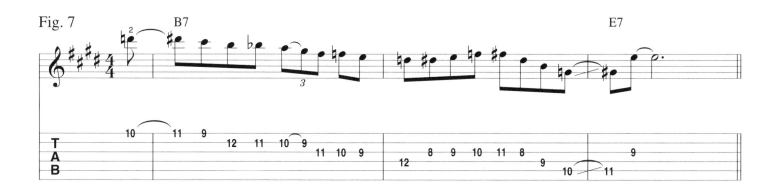

ROAD RUNNER

"Road Runner," is a fast, driving piece in the style of late 50s and early 60s rock, rhythm and blues but with a more modern guitar sound. It's split into three, six chorus sections, each building up to a climax and then returning to its opening dynamic level. Let these dynamics help you develop your ability to pace yourself and your ideas over a set period of time. Also note that the only difference between chorus 1 and chorus 2 is in the last measure where the music stops in chorus 2.

The sample scales for "Road Runner" include an extended fingering for A minor pentatonic (Fig. 2). This fingering can be used over any chord in the progression and allows you to move around the fingerboard without having to stop your ideas. Fig.1 , A minor blues, can also be used throughout the tune. Figs. 3, 4 and 5 are Mixolydian scales which should only be used over power chords with the same root (*i.e.*, E Mixolydian over E5). When using these scales it's important to remember that you can throw in passing tones now and then to get from one note to the next. Sliding into and out of notes is also an effective way to spice up your lines.

The first sample phrase (Fig. 6) begins with a large bend which must be held and re-picked several times before releasing. It's important to make sure you have enough fingers on the string you're bending, especially when it's a very wide bend such as in Fig. 6. Bending with only one finger is far more difficult than bending with two or three. Fig. 7 has a quirky rhythmic quality due to its use of triplets against a straight eighth-note feel. Fig. 7 is also specifically written to be used over the fourth, fifth, and sixth measures of the blues form only (D5 to A5). The last phrase, Fig. 8, is the most difficult so far. It's primarily based on an E7 arpeggio and should be practiced very slowly before trying to play it at full speed. Make sure you follow the left-hand fingering and slur markings for this lick.

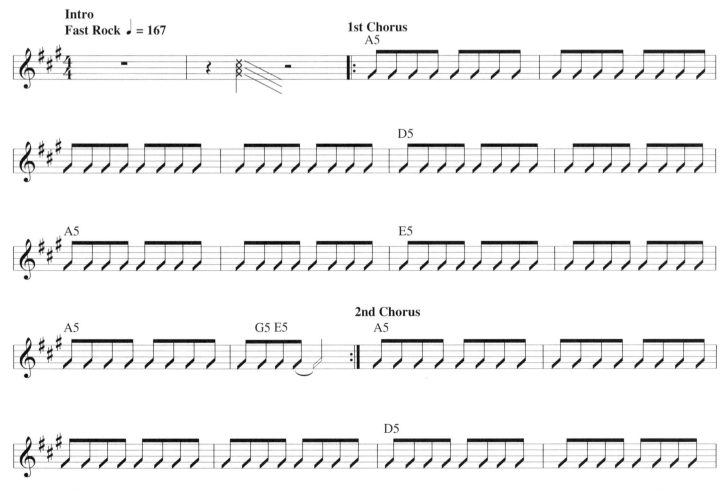

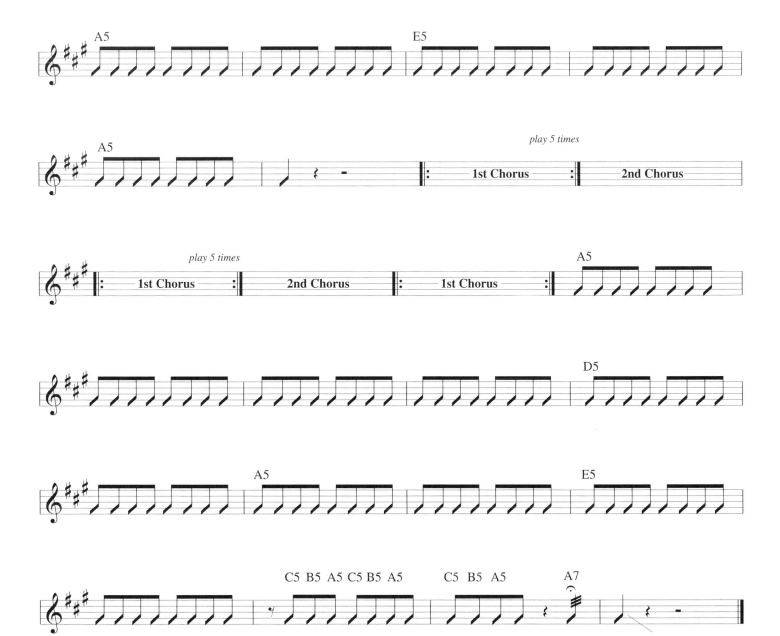

Scales for "Road Runner"

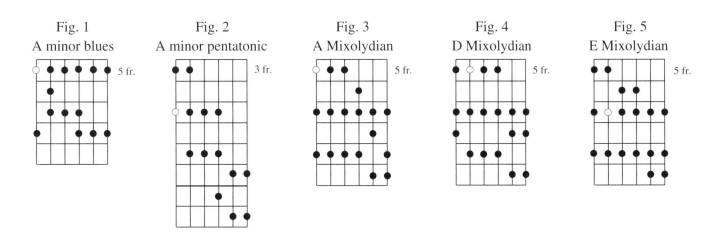

Fig. 1	Fig. 2	Fig. 3	Fig. 4	Fig. 5
A minor blues	A minor pentatonic	A Mixolydian	D Mixolydian	E Mixolydian

Sample Licks for "Road Runner"

Fig. 6

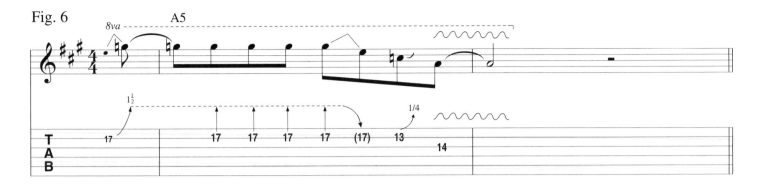

Fig. 7

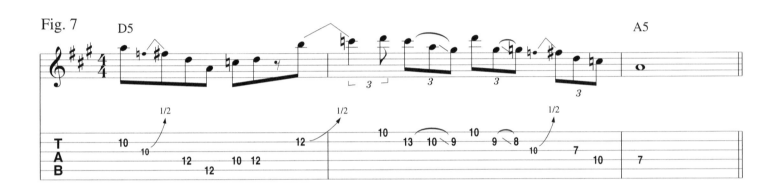

Fig. 8

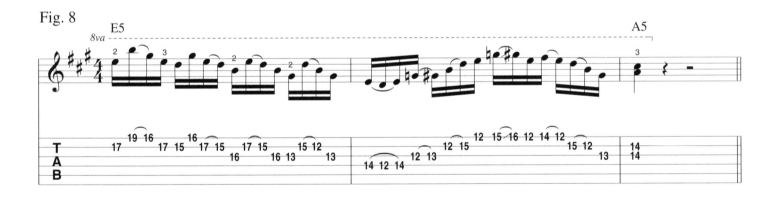

CHAPTER 2: COUNTRY JAMS

INTRODUCTION TO COUNTRY GUITAR

Country music has been a staple of American culture for nearly a century. Its simple chords, catchy melodies, toe-tapping beats and characteristic southern "twang" are instantly recognizable. The instrument featured most prominently in country music is the guitar. While its other stringed cousins — the banjo, mandolin, dobro, and pedal steel — are also important, the guitar (acoustic or electric) is still on top. Because of the guitar's important and diverse role in country music, it is necessary to be familiar with the various styles of this genre. Each one poses its own set of requirements and challenges for the country guitarist.

The audio and written music contained in this chapter are designed to teach you the skills necessary to become a proficient country player. Each tune addresses a different style, key and tempo used in modern country music and includes a chord chart, scale fingerings and a few sample lead phrases to help you develop and improve your improvising and technical ability. It is a good idea to look over the scale fingerings even if you think you know them already. The fingerings for each scale were specifically chosen to make improvising easier. They will often simplify your thought process and allow you to become more creative. It is also important for you to try the sample licks for each exercise. They will teach you various stylistic elements and give you a basic vocabulary of ideas that you can add to your own repertoire. (Note: The sample licks are performed at two speeds on the audio.)

As a final note, it is important for you to listen to as much country guitar playing as possible. There are many excellent recordings out there which can teach you new licks and inspire new ideas. One way to find these recordings is to read magazines and look at record reviews. It is also good to see and hear country artists in concert. The inspiration and insight gained from a live show is invaluable. Remember: learning anything worthwhile requires practice, patience and desire, so work hard and have fun with these country jams!

COWPOKE

"Cowpoke," is in the key of D major and has a laid back, medium-tempo swing feel. Most country songs use basic chords that are diatonic (related) to only one or two keys. These basic chords are primarily major and minor triads and dominant seventh chords. For this trune, the I, IV, and V chords (D, G and A) form the foundation of the harmony. This is a standard approach in country music. The only chord in the progression that is not diatonic to the key of D major is the E7 chord in the bridge. This chord is actually the V chord in the key of A major, so you'll have to switch scales when soloing over it.

The scales in Figs. 1-5 will help you improvise over each part of this exercise. Fig. 1 (D major blues) is a good choice to use against any D or G chord in the chart. Another option over the G chord is Fig. 2 (G major pentatonic). Fig. 3 (A major pentatonic) sounds good against any A or A7 chord in the chart. If you want to experiment with a few more notes, try using Fig. 4 (D major). Not every note in this scale will work perfectly all the time but if you practice the fingering and use your ear it will definitely make your phrases more colorful and interesting. The last scale, Fig. 5 (E Mixolydian), is the best choice to play over the E7 chord in the bridge. No other scale in Figs. 1-5 will sound as good.

Let's look at the sample licks in Figs. 6-8. Many of the licks in this chapter contain string bends which range from easy to very challenging. Because bending is an important part of country lead playing, it's a good idea to use lighter gauge strings (no heavier than a .010 for your high E string). The first lick (Fig. 6) is based on notes from the D major pentatonic scale. Make sure that you mute the B string during the release-bend of the first note in the second measure. The next lick (Fig. 7) begins with a "prebend." This is done by bending the string up before you pick it, then picking the string and releasing the bend. For the last lick (Fig. 8) you must bend and hold the G string up while picking several notes on the B string. Be sure to observe all the "let ring" markings in the tablature.

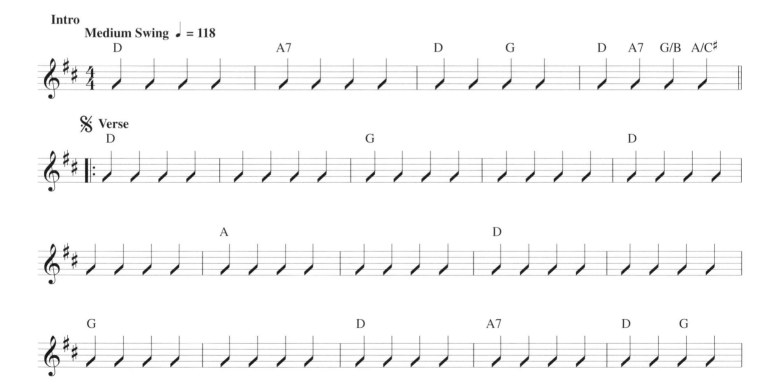

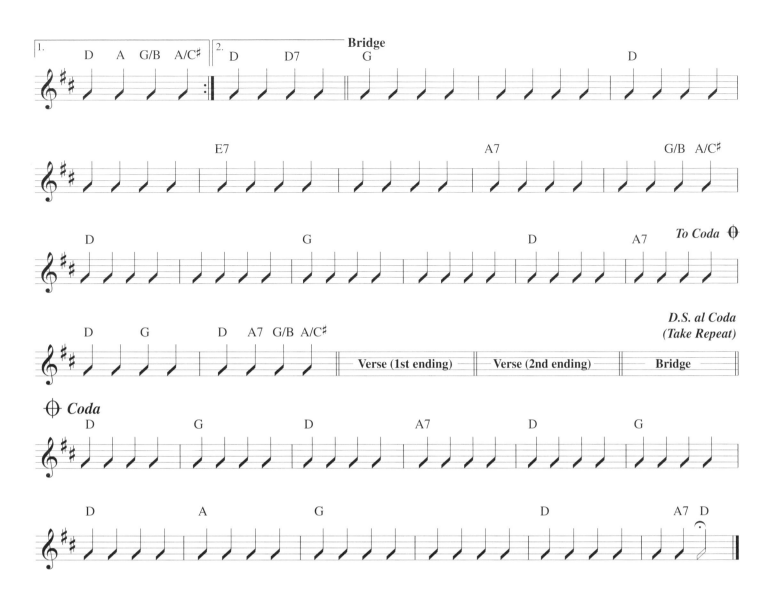

Scales for "Cowpoke"

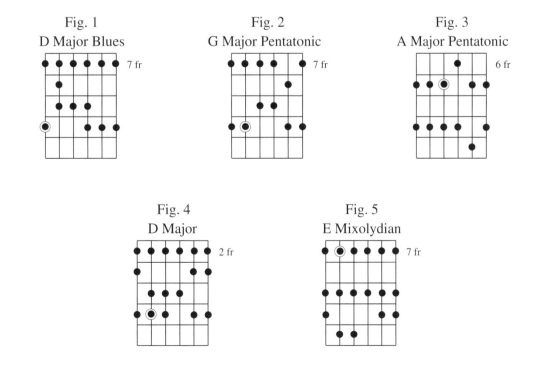

Fig. 1
D Major Blues
7 fr

Fig. 2
G Major Pentatonic
7 fr

Fig. 3
A Major Pentatonic
6 fr

Fig. 4
D Major
2 fr

Fig. 5
E Mixolydian
7 fr

Sample Licks for "Cowpoke"

Fig. 6

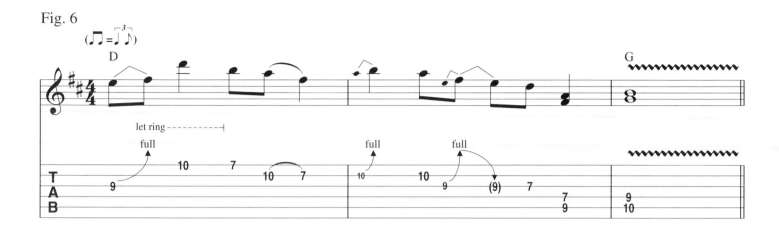

Fig. 7

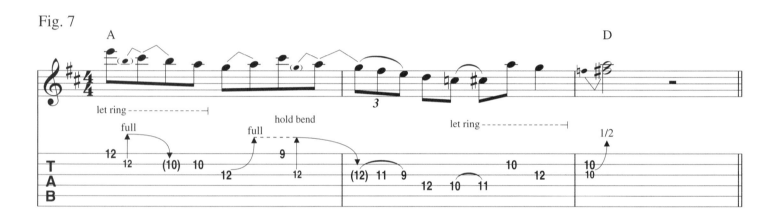

Fig. 8

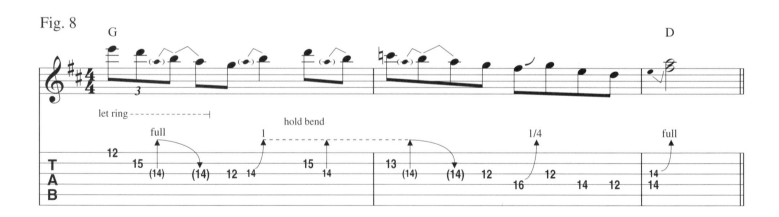

　　　　　　　　　　　　　　　　　　　　　　　　　　　　　　　　Cowpoke

TENNESSEE STRUT

"Tennessee Strut" is a 24-bar blues in C. The chord progression for this tune is somewhat different than a standard blues. In the verse, where a normal blues would go to the IV chord, this progression goes to a dominant ♭VII chord (B♭7), and instead of a V7 chord in the 17th measure, there is a dominant II chord (D7). The first suggested scale, Fig. 1 *(C minor blues)*, works very well over the intro and just about every measure of the chart except for measures seventeen and eighteen. For these measures, try using Fig. 5 *(D Mixolydian)*. The scales in Figs. 2, 3 and 4 work against any dominant seventh chord with the same root. For instance, Fig. 3 *(B♭ Mixolydian)* can be played against any B♭7 chord in the progression just as Fig. 4 *(F Mixolydian)* will work over any F7 chord.

The first sample phrase (Fig. 6) works over C7. It begins with a double bend which you must hold up while pulling off from the eighth fret to the sixth fret on the high E string. For the second lick (Fig. 7) it's important that you keep as many notes ringing together as possible. Doing this gives the phrase a pedal steel flavor, which is a common element in regular country guitar playing. The last lick (Fig. 8) is an exercise in first finger pull offs beginning with a three-note sequence rhythmically grouped in sixteenth notes. (The proper musical term for the open G note in this phrase is a "pedal tone".)

Scales for "Tennessee Strut"

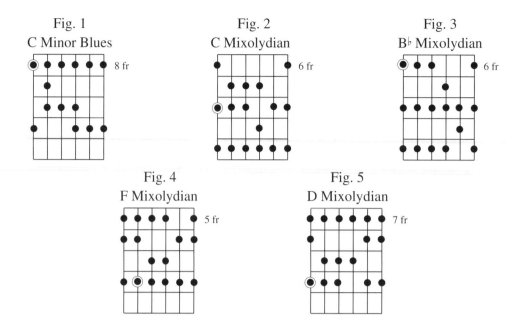

Fig. 1
C Minor Blues
8 fr

Fig. 2
C Mixolydian
6 fr

Fig. 3
B♭ Mixolydian
6 fr

Fig. 4
F Mixolydian
5 fr

Fig. 5
D Mixolydian
7 fr

Sample Licks for "Tennessee Strut"

Fig. 6

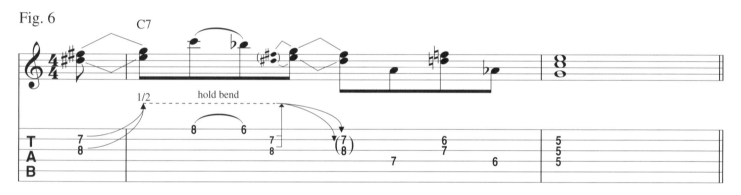

Fig. 7

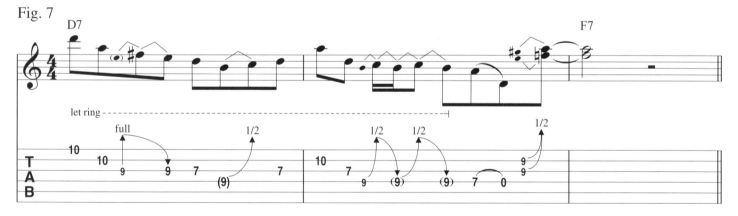

Fig. 8

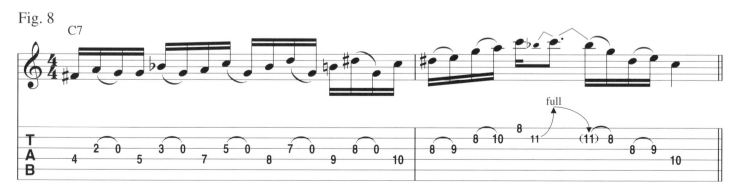

WHISKEY 'N' DIESEL

This tune is a medium tempo, bluesy shuffle in E with a strong, tight quarter-note feel. The primary scale choice for improvising is the *E minor blues* shown in Figs. 1 and 5. This scale sounds good over the entire progression, whereas the scales in Figs. 2, 3 and 4 will work only over specific chords. Fig. 2 *(A minor pentatonic)* is an optional scale choice for soloing over A7, just as Fig. 3 *(B minor pentatonic)* can be used over B7. Fig. 4 *(F♯ Mixolydian)* is the fifth mode in the key of B and can be used over any F♯7 chord in the progression.

The first two sample licks (Figs. 6 and 7) work over E7. Fig. 6 starts with a double bend on the B and G strings, but you want to only pick the G string initially. Fig. 7 uses *double stops* and intervals to create a funkier sound. A double stop is done by playing two strings with one finger and is a style used by many country players in solos and riffs. The final lick (Fig. 8) is a challenging stream of fast triplets. This phrase also contains many *chromatic passing tones* which smooth out the line and help add melodic tension. (A chromatic passing tone is a non-diatonic tone that connects two chord or scale tones. Although predominantly used in jazz, chromatic passing tones also find their way into other styles of music such as rock, blues and country.)

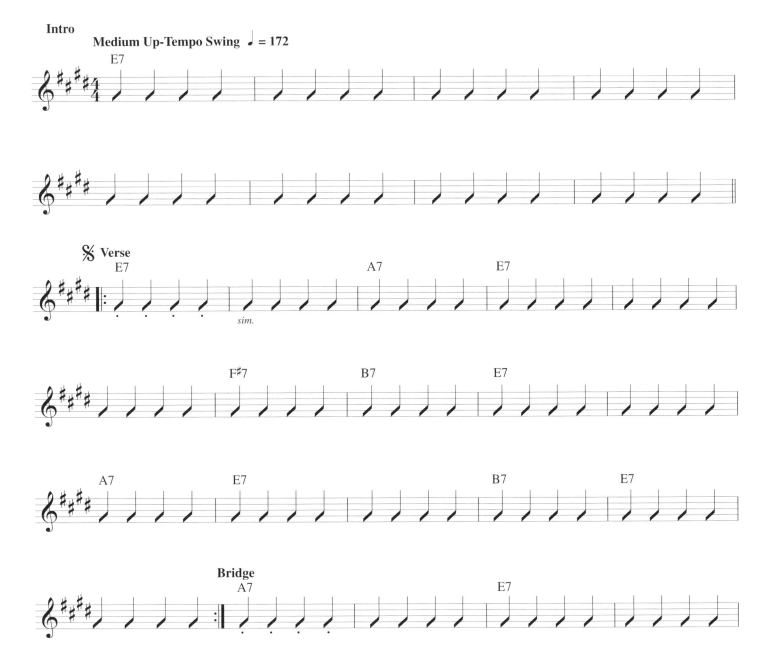

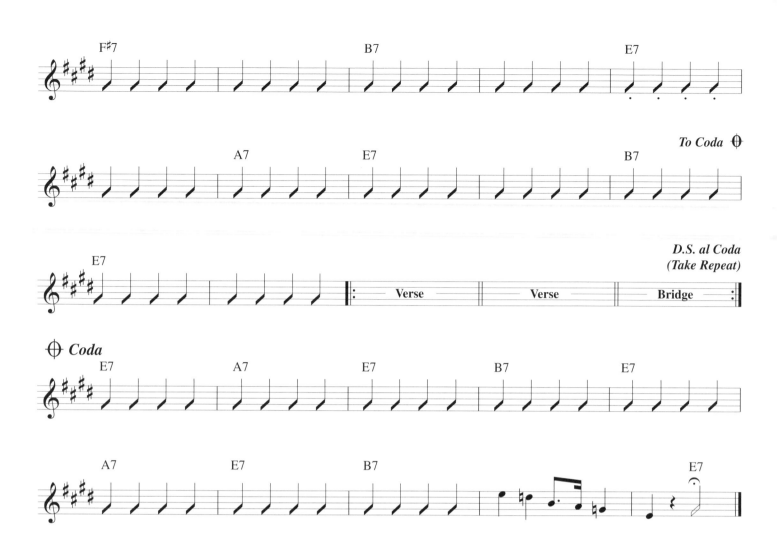

Scales for "Whiskey 'n' Diesel"

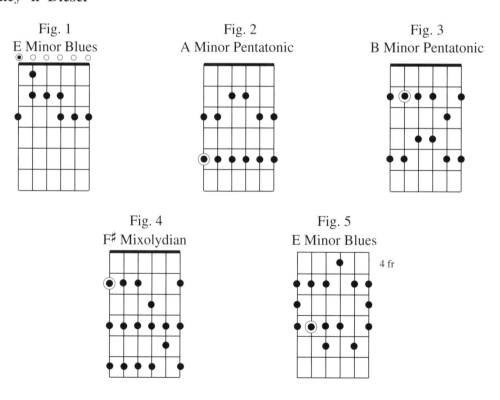

Fig. 1
E Minor Blues

Fig. 2
A Minor Pentatonic

Fig. 3
B Minor Pentatonic

Fig. 4
F# Mixolydian

Fig. 5
E Minor Blues

Sample Licks for "Whiskey 'n' Diesel"

Fig. 6

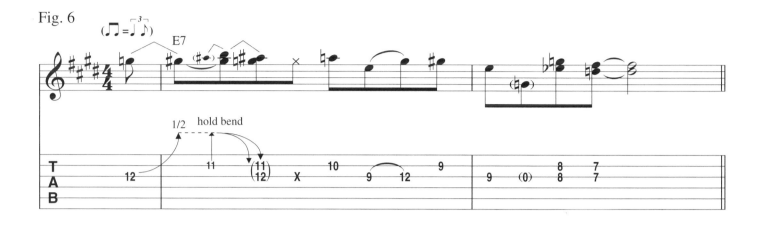

Fig. 7

Fig. 8

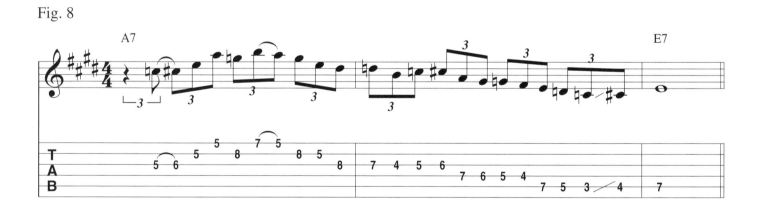

BARN BURNER

This is the most challenging of all the tunes in this chapter, due to the fast pace maintained throughout the song. Despite its tempo, "Barn Burner" is actually just a standard blues in A with a jazzy turnaround. The main scale for improvising is the *A minor blues* (Fig. 1). It works perfectly over every chord in the progression. The other scales given for this exercise address specific chords. Fig. 2 *(A major blues)* is a nice choice over A7, while *D major pentatonic* and *E major pentatonic* work against D7 and E7, respectively. Figs. 5 and 6 are actually not scales but *arpeggios*. An arpeggio is sounded by separately playing the notes of a chord. Fig. 5 is an F♯7 arpeggio and Fig. 6 a B7 arpeggio. You may find it difficult to address each chord individually at first, but with a little practice your ear and fingers will be ready to take on the challenge.

The first phrase (Fig. 7) works against an A7 chord and begins with a fiddle-like motif that switches to a series of open string pull-offs. The next lick (Fig. 8) involves sliding and bending to create a pedal steel effect over the E7 to D7 chord change. The trick in Fig. 8 is to bend the string up as quickly as possible after you've slid into the next position. (Remember not to pick the notes that have slur markings going to them.) The final lick (Fig. 9) is a little confusing at first, but not terribly difficult to play once you memorize the position changes. The entire phrase works over the IV7 chord (D7) and starts with some tricky open string pull-offs. The first position change is on the sixth note of the second measure (D). This note should be played with your first finger.

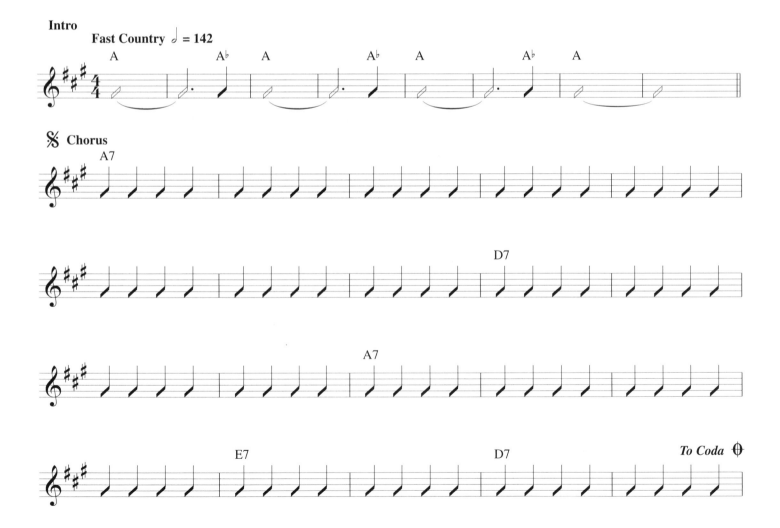

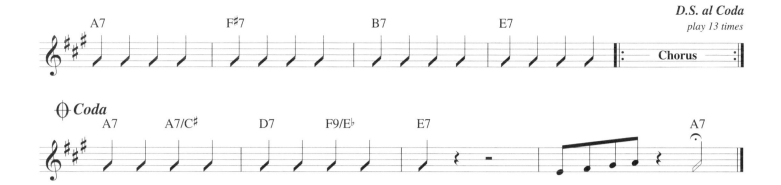

Scales for "Barn Burner"

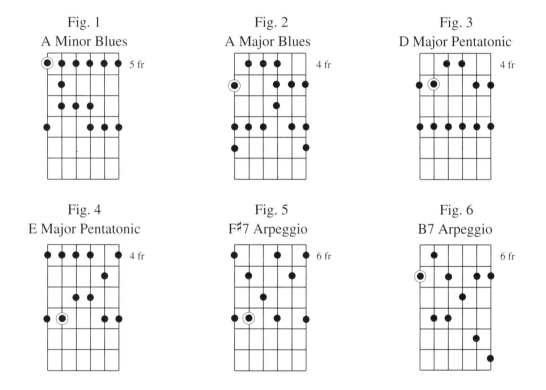

Sample Licks for "Barn Burner"

Fig. 7

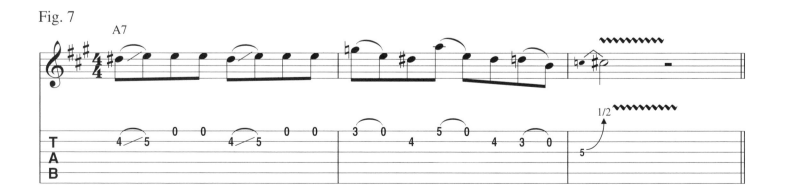

Fig. 8

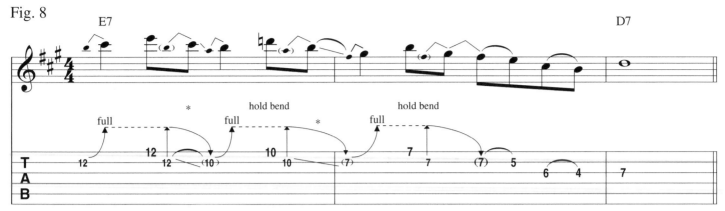

* Release bend and slide simultaneously.

Fig. 9

SOUTHERN BELLE

Southern Belle is a slow ballad with a straight eighth-note feel. It is in the key of B major and is one of the easier tunes to improvise over. The only chord that presents a challenge is the C♯7 chord in the sixth measure of the bridge. Fig. 4 *(C♯ Mixolydian)* is the best choice for addressing this chord. You can improvise over the rest of the progression with the *B major* (Fig. 1) and *B major pentatonic* (Fig. 2) scales. Figs. 3 and 5 will work over all F♯ chords.

It is often customary on country ballads for the pedal steel player to handle the soloing duties. However, guitarists can create their own convincing pedal steel effects by using bends, harmonics and other techniques. The first lick (Fig. 6) contains a somewhat unorthodox technique for country guitar: tapping! Tapping is predominantly used in rock and heavy metal, but here it is used in a country setting to enhance the release of a double bend on the B and G strings. The second phrase (Fig. 7) also has many pedal steel-like qualities. It's very important in Fig. 7 to make sure all the notes ring out together or the effect will be lost. Fig. 8 is one of the most deceptively challenging licks in this chapter. On paper it looks easy, but it requires tremendous hand strength and control to execute properly. The trick to playing Fig. 8 is to begin by bending the G string up before picking any of the harmonics. The harmonics should be performed by holding the pick between your thumb and middle finger and touching the string with the index finger of your picking hand twelve frets above whatever note(s) you're holding down with your fretting hand. By picking the string while your index finger is touching it, you will hear a harmonic one octave above the note your left hand is fretting. When playing this lick, make sure to keep every note ringing throughout the phrase.

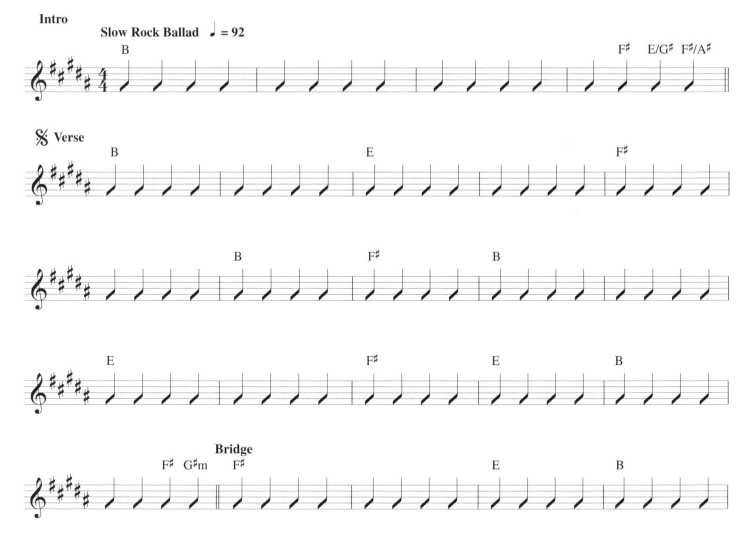

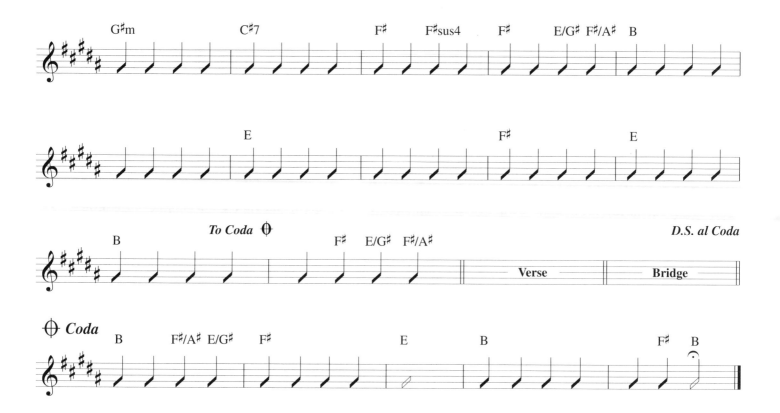

Scales for "Southern Belle"

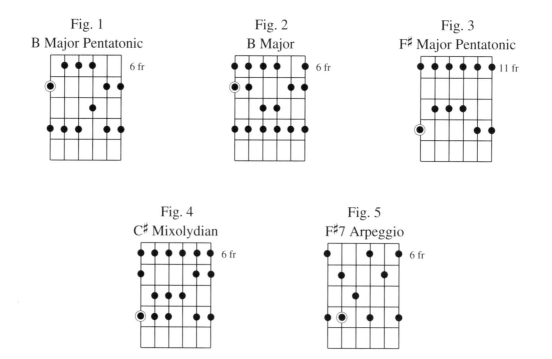

Fig. 1
B Major Pentatonic
6 fr

Fig. 2
B Major
6 fr

Fig. 3
F♯ Major Pentatonic
11 fr

Fig. 4
C♯ Mixolydian
6 fr

Fig. 5
F♯7 Arpeggio
6 fr

Sample Licks for "Southern Belle"

Fig. 6

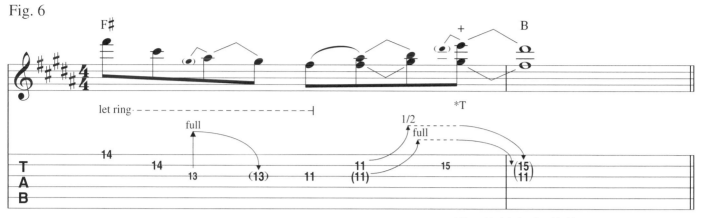

* Tap with right hand and hold note
while releasing bend with left hand.

Fig. 7

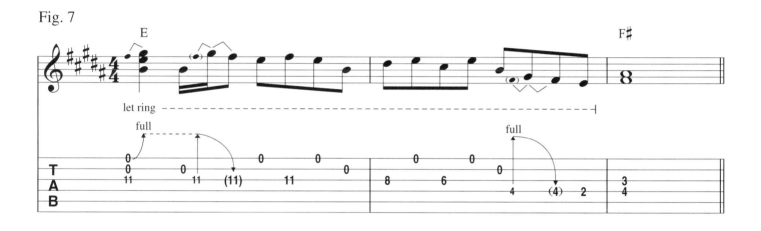

Fig. 8

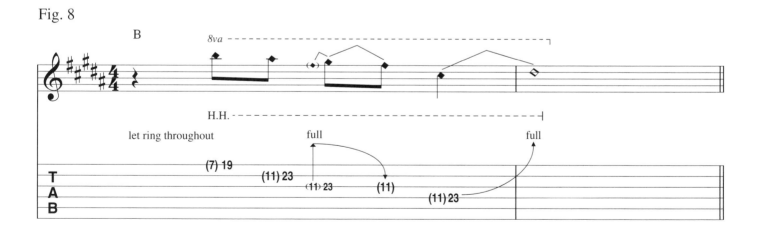

PROMENADE

"Promenade" is a medium tempo, swing tune in G major. There are no key changes so you can use one scale throughout. Figs. 1, 2, 3 and 4 all work equally well over the entire progression. After you've learned the suggested scales, try playing them twelve frets lower than where they're written. Also try experimenting with *passing tones* and other notes outside of the notes given for each scale. These notes can help create melodic tension and add more complexity to your lines.

The sample phrase in Fig. 5 is reminiscent of a banjo technique called a "roll." Make sure you let every string ring out as long as possible. Fig. 6 is a traditional country ending lick and should be used at the very end of the tune on the last two measures of the coda section. Before you play the first note of Fig. 6, start by silently bending the G string up a whole step at the fourteenth fret. The last phrase works over the very beginning of the progression. It is important to keep the first note bent up a half step while playing the other notes in the first measure.

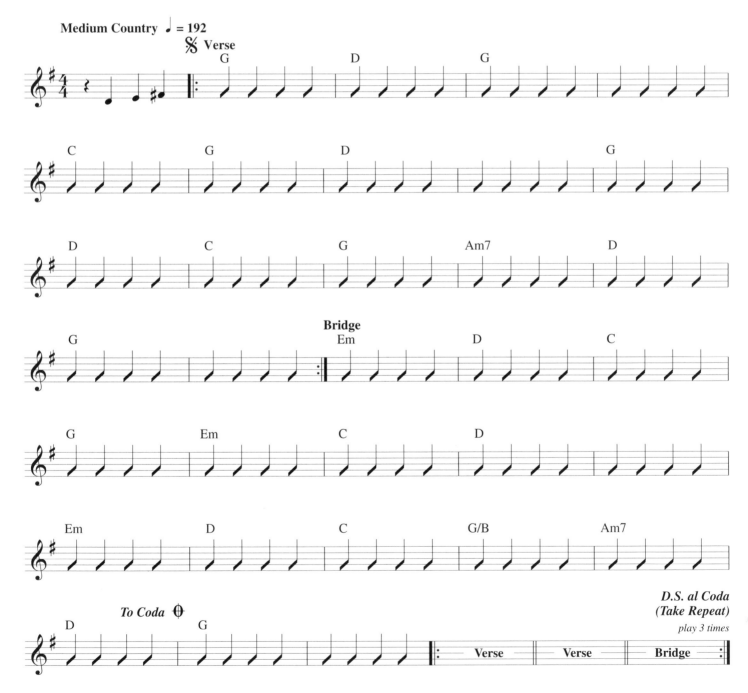

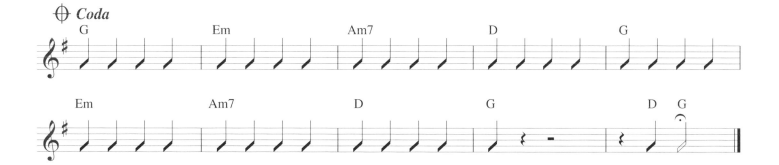

Scales for "Promenade"

Fig. 1	Fig. 2	Fig. 3	Fig. 4
G Major Blues	G Major	G Minor Blues	G Major Pentatonic

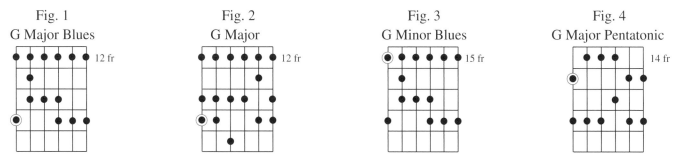

Sample Licks for "Promenade"

Fig. 5

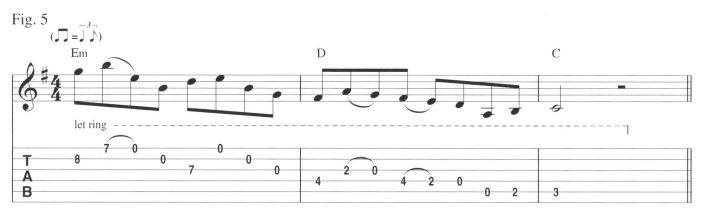

Fig. 6

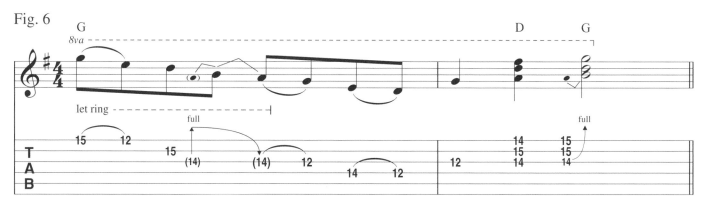

Fig. 7

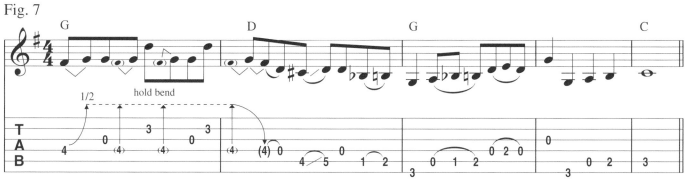

HOMESTEAD

This tune is an example of a slow country waltz. A waltz is characterized by its 3/4 time signature and accent on the first beat of each measure. Most of this exercise is in the key of F major with the exception of the sixth measure of the bridge (G7). Over the G7 chord you can use the *G Mixolydian* scale shown in Fig. 3. For the rest of the progression, use Fig. 1 *(F major)* and Fig. 2 *(F major pentatonic)*.

The first lick (Fig. 4) contains a triple bend. When performing this, it is very important that you bend the B and G strings a whole step and the D string only a half step. The second lick (Fig. 5) works over the bridge. It begins with a sequence of grace note hammer-ons and resolves by sustaining one string while bending another. The final phrase (Fig. 6) works over measures 5-7 or 13-15. Make sure you hold the first note of this lick for the entire first measure.

Scales for "Homestead"

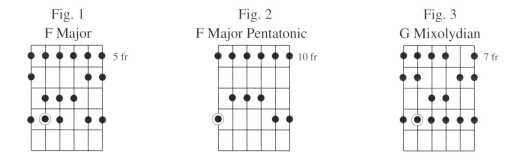

Fig. 1
F Major

Fig. 2
F Major Pentatonic

Fig. 3
G Mixolydian

Sample Licks for "Homestead"

Fig. 4

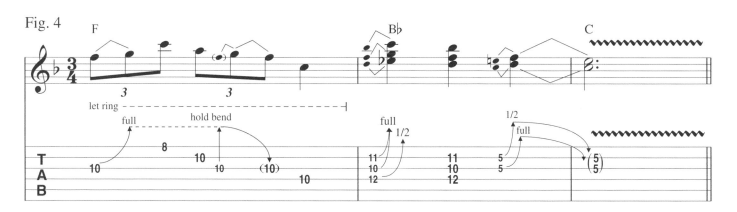

Fig. 5

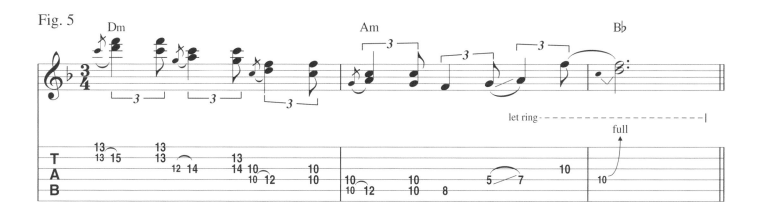

Fig. 6

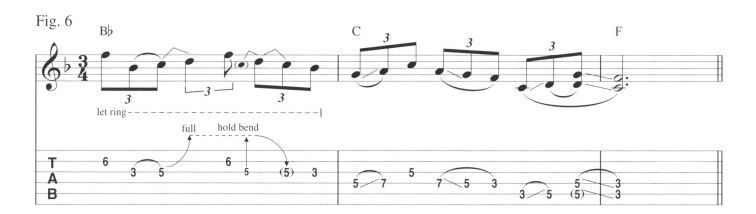

WESTERN SUNSET

"Western Sunset" is a medium tempo, straight eighth-note groove reminiscent of some of the Eagles' work from the seventies. The entire progression is in the key of G major, with the exception of the G7 chord in the tenth measure of the bridge. Figs. 1, 2 and 3 are all fingerings for the *G major pentatonic* scale and can be used over any part of the chart. The *G major* scale in Fig. 4 can also be used over the entire progression except for the G7 chord. The best scale to use against the G7 chord is the *G Mixolydian* in Fig. 5 because it contains the note F natural, which is part of the G7 chord.

Fig. 6 is designed to work over the last two measures of the bridge. Be sure to let notes ring where indicated. Fig. 7 starts with a pedal steel-type bend that involves bending the G string up a whole step and then releasing it in precise half-step increments. The last lick (Fig. 8) is somewhat challenging. It begins with a prebend that leads into a whole step bend on the D string. This must be held while playing notes on the G and B strings. It ends with a pull off to your first finger which you must simultaneously bend up a half step and then release.

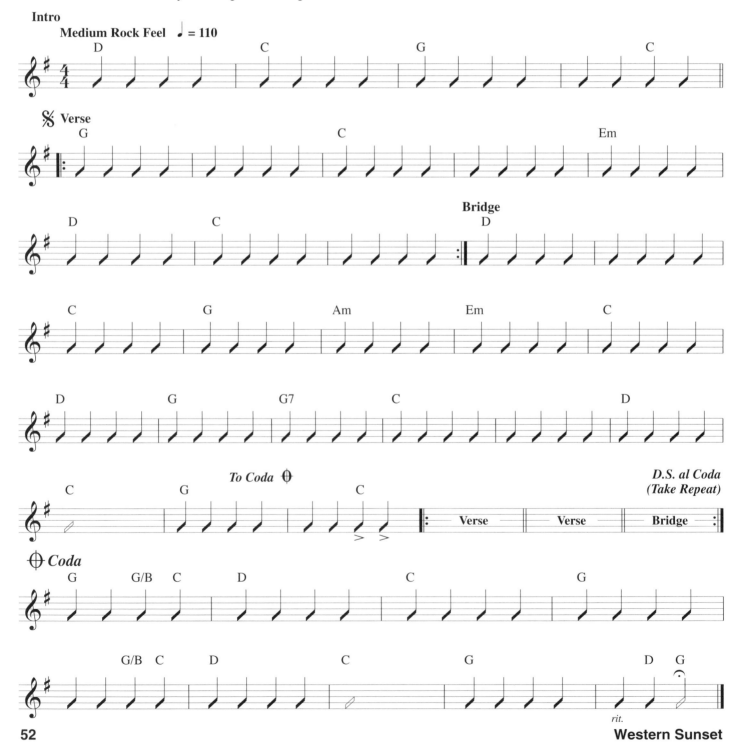

     Western Sunset

Scales for "Western Sunset"

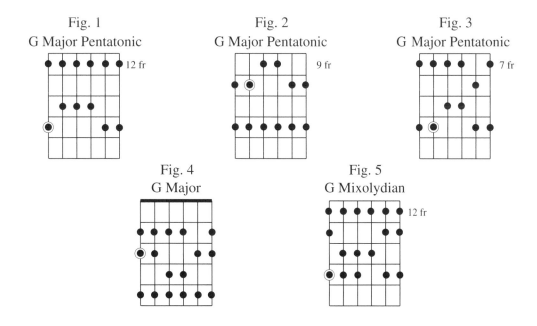

Fig. 1
G Major Pentatonic
12 fr

Fig. 2
G Major Pentatonic
9 fr

Fig. 3
G Major Pentatonic
7 fr

Fig. 4
G Major

Fig. 5
G Mixolydian
12 fr

Sample Licks for "Western Sunset"

Fig. 6

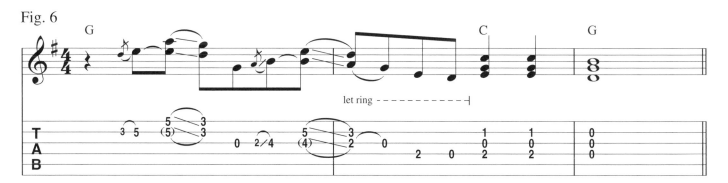

Fig. 7

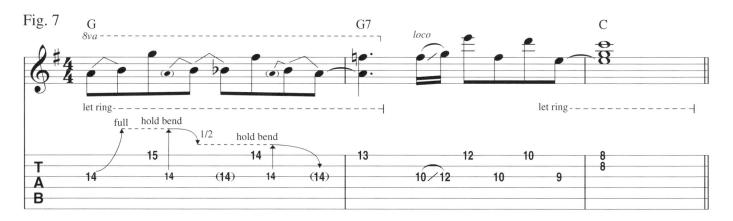

Fig. 8

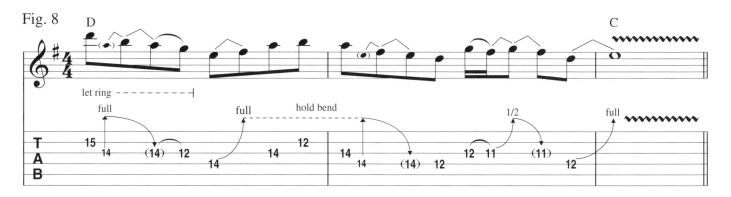

ROPIN' AND RIDIN'

This tune is an elongated blues in D with a fast rock feel. The *D minor blues* scale in Fig. 1 can be used over the whole chart. The scales in Figs. 2, 3 and 4 work over specific chords: Fig. 2 (*G major blues*) is an optional scale for any G or G7 chord, Fig. 3 (*A minor blues*) is an optional scale for A or A7, and Fig. 4 (*B♭ Mixolydian*) is a good choice to use over any B♭7 chords in the progression.

Let's look at the sample licks. Fig. 5 starts with an eighth-note pick up and works against all D7 chords. The last measure resolves in an interesting way with three intervals moving in contrary motion. The second phrase (Fig. 6) works over the first four bars of the bridge (G7-D7). The key in Fig. 6 is to hold and let ring as many notes as possible during the first two measures. The last lick (Fig. 7) is potentially the most challenging in this chapter. It is based on techniques pioneered and de-veloped by the great Jerry Donahue who is famous for his incredible string bending ability. One of his most amazing techniques is his two string contrary motion bend, where he's able to make two strings bend in opposite directions simultaneously. This is done by pulling one string down, then catching an adjacent string under your finger, and pushing both strings back up. Fig. 7 begins by pulling the G string down with your first finger (towards the B string). You then catch the B string so that both strings are now under your finger, and finish the lick by pushing both strings up, so that the B string is bending up a half step while the G string is being released a whole step. This happens again between the D and G strings a beat later. (Be sure to obey all the "let ring" and "hold bend" markings in the tablature.)

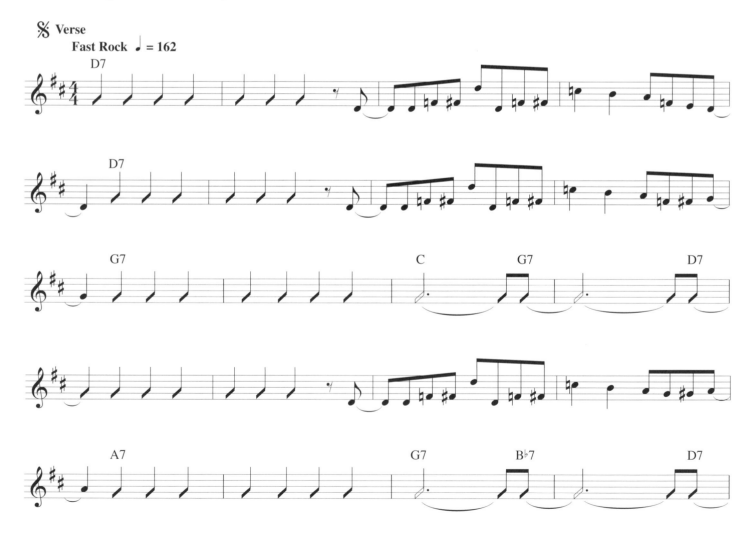

Scales for "Ropin' and Ridin'"

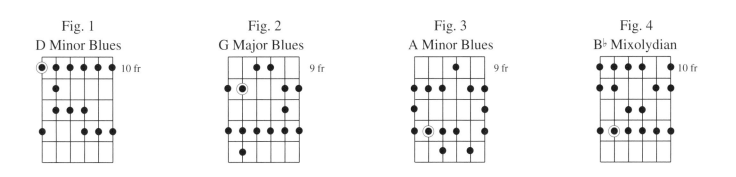

Fig. 1
D Minor Blues
10 fr

Fig. 2
G Major Blues
9 fr

Fig. 3
A Minor Blues
9 fr

Fig. 4
B♭ Mixolydian
10 fr

Sample Licks for "Ropin' and Ridin'"

Fig. 5

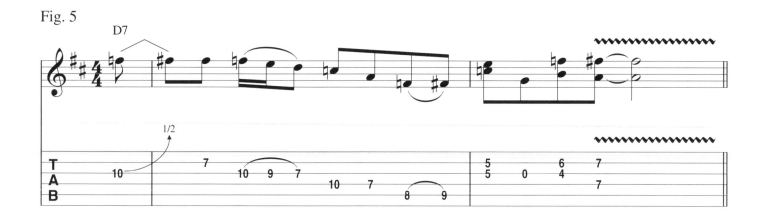

Fig. 6

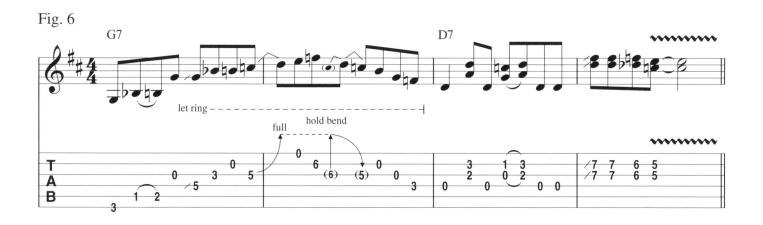

Fig. 7

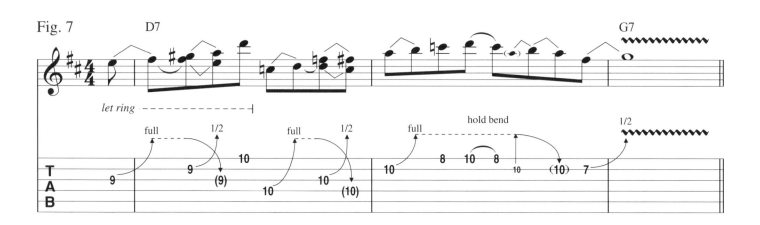

🔊 HONKY TONK SHUFFLE

The title of this tune says it all: a medium tempo, bluesy shuffle in A. Actually, the form for this chart is not a strict blues. The verse behaves like a standard twelve bar blues up to the tenth measure but then extends the V chord (in this case E7) for two more measures before resolving back to the I chord (A7). The entire verse is repeated and then moves on to an eight bar bridge. After the bridge go back to the verse and play through the form all over again.

The main scale for this exercise is the *A blues* shown in Fig. 1. It can be used over any part of the progression. Fig. 2 *(A major blues)* and Fig. 3 *(A Mixolydian)* should be used over only A7 chords, while Fig. 4 *(B Mixolydian,)* works over the B7 chord in the bridge. For all E7 chords you can use the E7 arpeggio fingering given in Fig. 5.

The first lick (Fig. 6) works against any A7 chord in the piece and utilizes notes from both the *A major* and *A minor blues* scales. The second lick (Fig. 7) is a bit faster and employs some challenging open string pull-offs. Be sure you observe all articulation markings when practicing this one. The last phrase (Fig. 7) is a diatonic sequence in sixths. Note that this lick begins on an eighth note pick-up into the first measure, not directly on beat one.

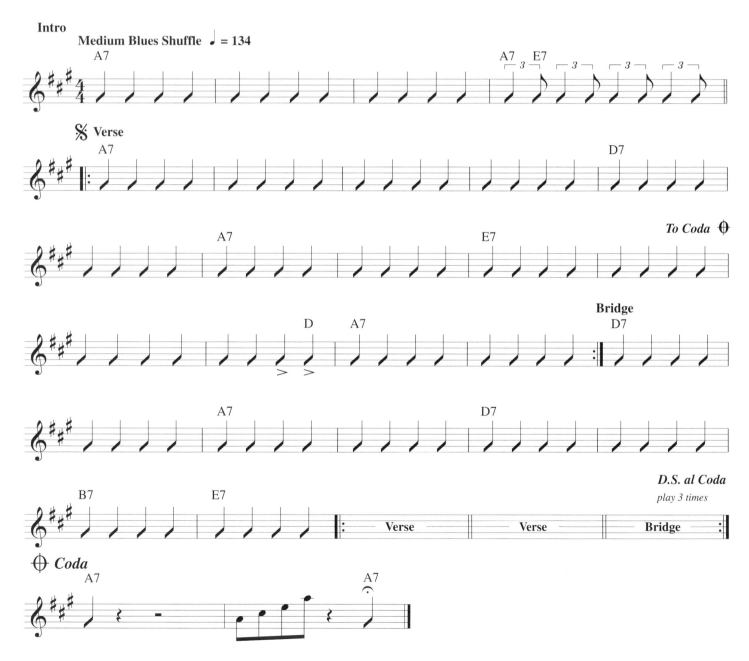

Scales for "Honky Tonk Shuffle"

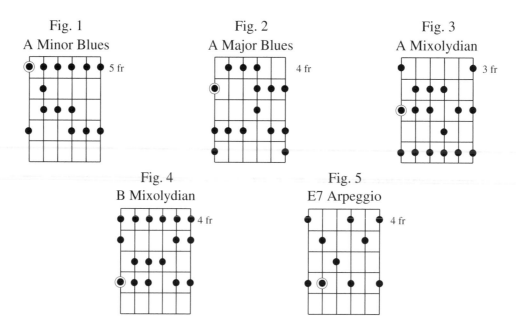

Sample Licks for "Honky Tonk Shuffle"

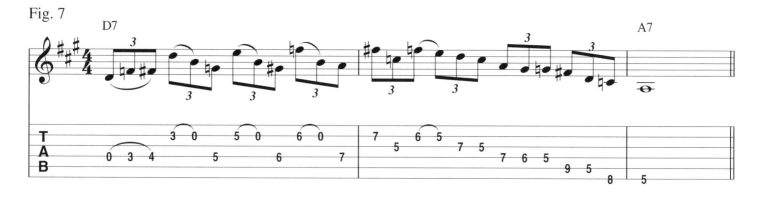

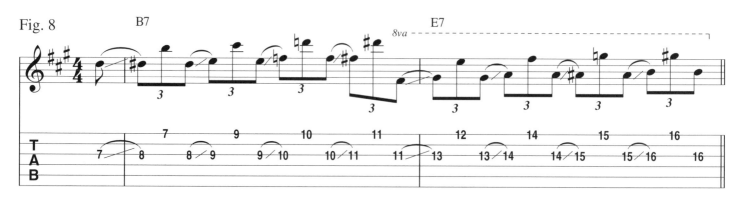

CHAPTER 3: FUNK JAMS

INTRODUCTION TO FUNK GUITAR

Funk is not so much a style of music as it is a *feel*. It is difficult to say what makes music feel funky. As a general rule, it is based around the sixteenth note, either straight or swung. However, formal music terms are not really adequate in defining why something "grooves" or doesn't. In the past, funk as been described with vague words and phrases such as "relaxed," "groovin'," "locked up" or "in the pocket," but none of these descriptions mean much unless you've played with a funk band which had the audience on its feet.

It's important when learning any style that you listen to as many good examples of it as possible. This includes buying recordings as well as going to live shows. Some of the great pioneers of funk music include James Brown, Sly and the Family Stone, Booker T and the MGs, George Clinton and Parliament, The Meters, The Isley Brothers, Kool and the Gang, Earth, Wind and Fire, Tower of Power and many, many others. While some of these bands are still recording and performing, much of the funk music that's written today comes from rap and hip hop artists, so check them out too.

As you play with these tracks, listen to how the various instruments interact without getting in each other's way. Especially listen to the drums and bass, which are the foundation of every great band. Be aware of all the accents that are played or implied by the band and how repeated parts are varied and developed. Also remember that the soloist has as much responsibility for making the groove happen as the rhythm section. Playing funk is a group effort and all the pieces must lock together or the groove dies. The primary consideration of every funk musician is to make people want to get up and move to the beat.

The last important point that should be made is that although these jam lessons are generally designed to help you master single-note soloing and improvising, in a funk band a guitarist's main job is to play tasty, funky *rhythm* parts. This is why the sample phrases for each track include one example of a rhythm guitar idea. If you burn the audio on a CD and listen through a stereo system, turn the right channel all the way off. This will remove the guitar parts that are on each track and allow you to practice your own rhythm parts.

BACK TO THE BAY

"Back to the Bay" is a James Brown/Tower of Power inspired track based around a 24 bar C blues progression. The progression is similar to a normal 12 bar blues, except each chord lasts twice as long. There is also a substitute II7 chord (D9) in the 17th and 18th measures where the V7 (G7) chord would normally be. The scales in Figs. 1 and 2 (*C blues*) work over the entire progression except for the substitute II7 chord (D9). Try using Fig. 3 (*D dominant pentatonic over the D9 chord*). Also practice starting an idea in one scale and ending it in another. This is particularly important when improvising from the 16th into the 17th measure.

This tune is one of the "busiest" rhythmically. All of the instruments are simultaneously playing ideas based on "straight" (or even) sixteenth notes. It works because each instrument leaves "pockets of space," freeing other instruments to fill the gaps. This allows the music to "breathe" and prevents it from sounding too cluttered or muddy. When you play along, try using short, syncopated rhythms in your solos to enhance the funkiness of the tune.

All of the sample phrases for "Back to the Bay" work over C9. The first one (Fig. 4) is a two measure rhythm guitar idea employing double-stops and sliding intervals. Make sure that you mute out all the strings with your left hand when indicated. Fig. 5 introduces *quarter-step bends*. A quarter-step bend is executed by bending (a string) a tiny amount so that the final sounding pitch is somewhere above the original note but less than a half step. If it sounds slightly out of tune to your ear, you're doing it right! The resulting sound creates tension and is very popular in both funk and blues guitar playing. The final lick (Fig. 6) uses several arpeggios connected together to outline the C9 chord.

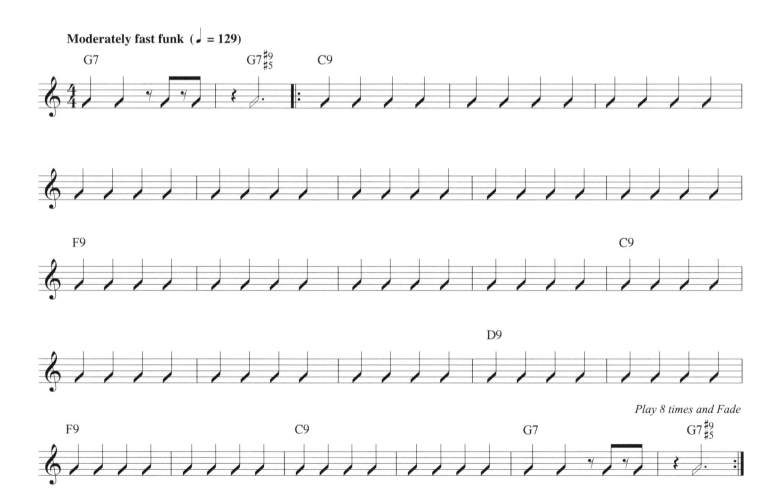

Scales for "Back to the Bay"

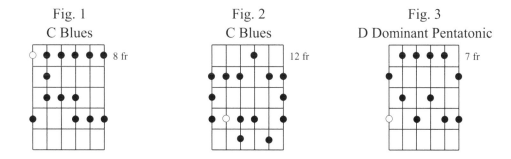

Fig. 1	Fig. 2	Fig. 3
C Blues	C Blues	D Dominant Pentatonic

Samples Licks for "Back to the Bay"

Fig. 4

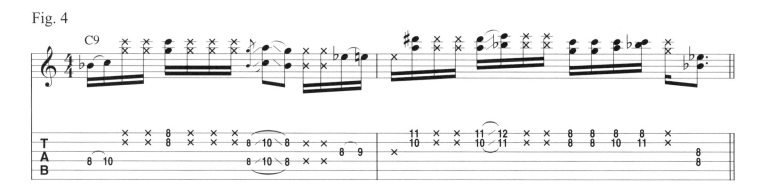

Fig. 5

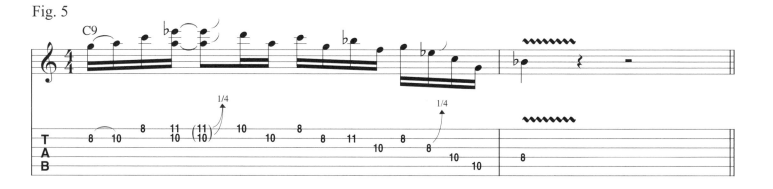

Fig. 6

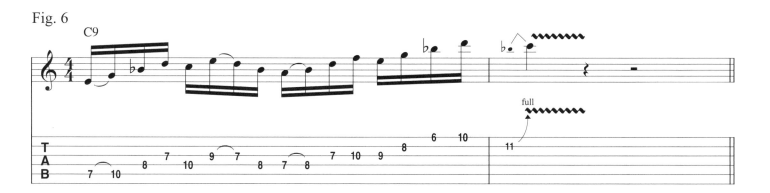

FLIP FLOP

"Flip Flop" is primarily constructed around the key of E minor. Consequently, you may use Figs. 1 and 2 (*E blues* and *E Dorian*) over the entire tune, except for the bridge. Here, the music changes to an A Dorian tonality, and as a result, you must change scales. The *A Dorian* scale shown in Fig. 3 is a sensible choice because it's written in the same position as Figs. 1 and 2 so you won't have to move all over the neck to find it. An optional scale, *B Spanish Phrygian* has been provided in Fig. 4. This can be used over the B7♯5 chord in the fourth measure of the chorus. However, if this scale is not comfortable for you, just stick with Fig. 1 (E blues).

Rhythmically this exercise has a "hip hop" feel. This means that each beat is divided into four "swing" sixteenth-note pulses. To understand this better, imagine dividing each beat into four even pulses and then make the 2nd and 4th pulses occur slightly later than normal. This means that the 1st and 3rd pulses are longer in value than the 2nd and 4th.

The first sample phrase (Fig. 5) is a rhythm guitar idea that works over the verse. The way to make this lick sound funky is to keep your picking hand moving up and down at all times. The "X"s in notation and tab indicate where left hand muting should occur. Figs. 6 and 7 are lead phrases that work against any part of the track that's based around Em7 (such as the verse, chorus and breakdown). Fig. 7 begins with a bend at the 19th fret which you must then simultaneously release and slide down from.

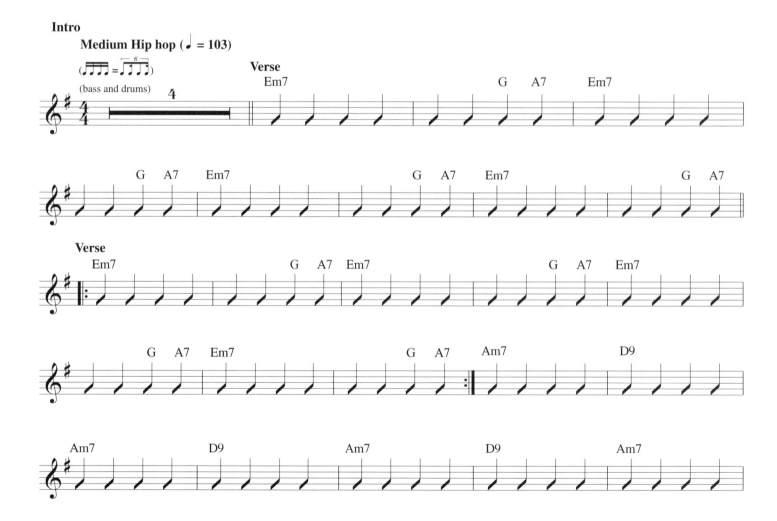

Flip Flop

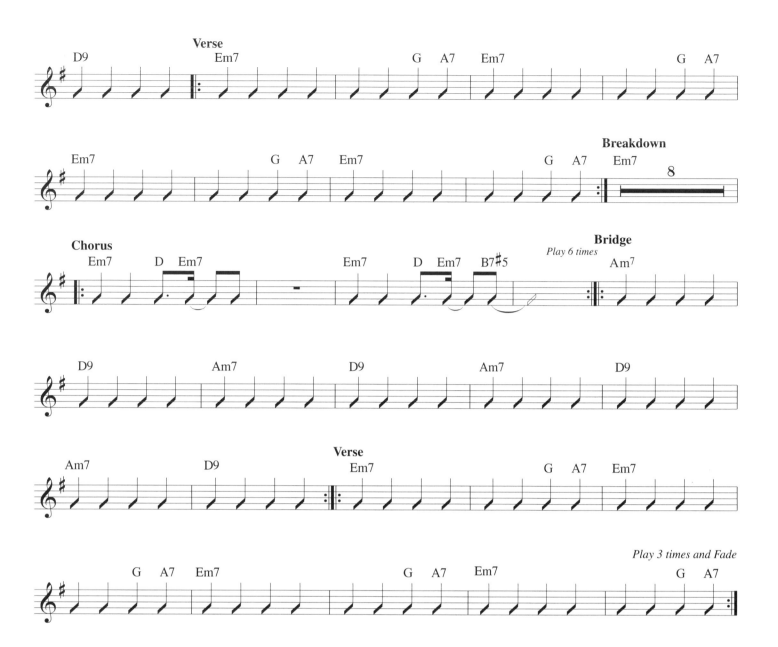

Scales for "Flip Flop"

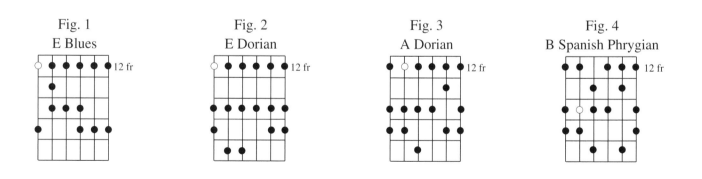

Fig. 1
E Blues

Fig. 2
E Dorian

Fig. 3
A Dorian

Fig. 4
B Spanish Phrygian

Samples Licks for "Flip Flop"

Fig. 5

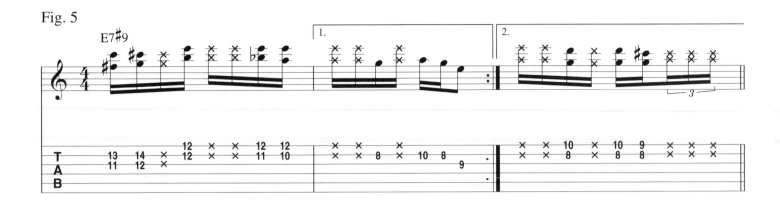

Fig. 6

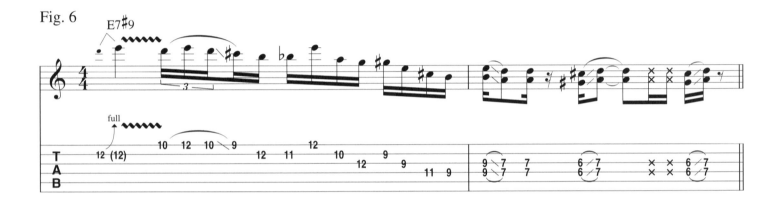

Fig. 7

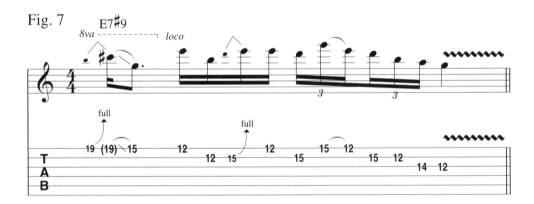

MARACHINO

"Marachino" is a '70s influenced funk tune similar in feel to "Play That Funky Music" by the group Wild Cherry. Most of the chart is built around the F Dorian scale (Fig. 1) with the exception of the bridge. During the bridge you must alternate between *D♭ Mixolydian* (Fig. 2) over the D♭9 chord and F Dorian over Fm7. Another approach to improvising on the bridge is to use the A♭ *Kamoi* scale (Fig. 3) over the D♭9 chord and *F minor pentatonic scale* (Fig. 4) against the Fm7 chord. You can think of the A♭ Kamoi scale as an F minor pentatonic scale with a C♭ instead of a C.

The feel of this exercise is a medium tempo, straight sixteenth-note groove. This means that each beat is divided into four even sixteenth notes or sub-beats. A good way to approach rhythm playing for this track would be to start by moving your picking hand down and up in a constant motion over the strings without touching them. Your pick should cross the strings four times for each beat (i.e., down-up-down-up) in sync with the sixteenth-notes. Now pick a suitable chord or note for the section you're playing against (most likely an Fm7 chord). Without stopping your picking hand, lower it into the strings on beats on and three only. On beats two and four pull it away from the strings. Now try the whole thing again, but this time instead of pulling your picking hand away on beats two and four, leave it in place and mute the strings with your fretting hand. Try this a few times using various rhythms with your fretting hand and keeping your picking hand moving at all times.

The lick in Fig. 5 is a two measure rhythm idea you can use over the verse or Fm7 chord. The first measure utilizes a chord embellishment by pulling off the note D to C. In the context of the Fm7 harmony, this creates the movement to Fm13 changing to Fm7. The second measure begins with a series of double-stops which should be played by barring so that both notes are being played by one finger. The next lick, note (Fig. 6) also works against the Fm7 chord and involves position changes and tricky first finger bends. The last phrase (Fig. 7) is interesting because it's a six-note sequence that begins "inside" the harmony, then goes "outside," and then comes back inside at the end.

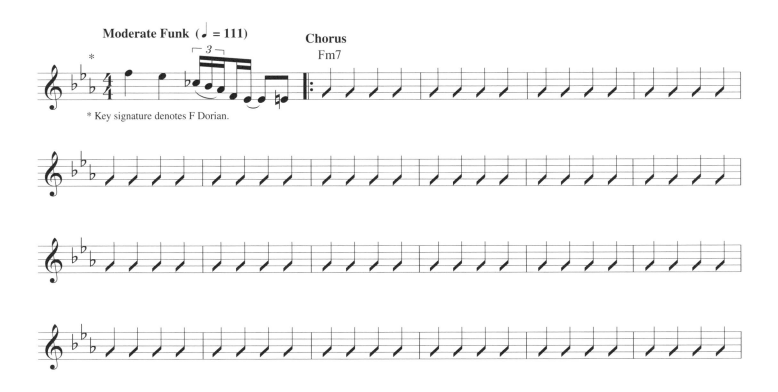

Moderate Funk (♩ = 111)

Chorus

Fm7

* Key signature denotes F Dorian.

Scales for "Marachino"

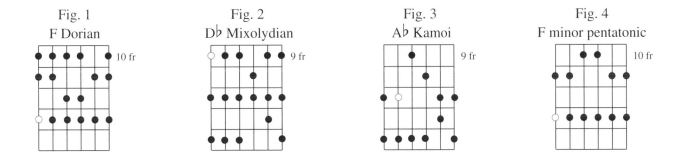

Fig. 1
F Dorian

Fig. 2
D♭ Mixolydian

Fig. 3
A♭ Kamoi

Fig. 4
F minor pentatonic

Samples Licks for "Marachino"

Fig. 5

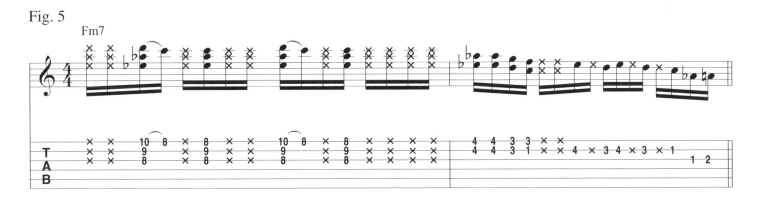

Fig. 6

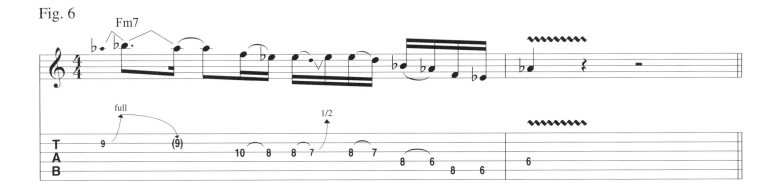

Fig. 7

METRIC

"Metric" is a tune heavily influenced by the great New Orleans funk band, The Meters. Their sound and style was highly unique, employing quirky, syncopated rhythms in a pop/funk context. The verse section is based around the *A Mixolydian* scale (Fig. 1). You can also use the A Mixolydian scale in conjunction with the *A blues* scale in Fig. 2 for improvising over the verse, interlude, and open vamp on A7. The bridge is based around the *D Mixolydian* scale shown in Fig. 3, which means you must switch scales at that point. You also use the *D blues* scale (Fig. 4) during the bridge.

The feel of this exercise is based on "swing" sixteenth notes. If you listen closely to the drum part during the verse, you'll notice how it seems to pull the music back and forth. This is achieved through "syncopation" or by accenting what are normally considered weak pulses by the snare and bass drum. A good example of this is the periodic emphasis of the "and" after beat 3 during the first, third, fifth, and ninth measures of the verse. This has the effect of stopping the beat dead in its tracks only to have it jump forward again in the next measure. Try to take advantage of this syncopated feel during the verse when you are improvising. Contrast it with the more straight-ahead, backbeat-driven feel of the bridge and interlude.

Fig. 5 is a rhythm guitar part that works over A7. The entire phrase is played in fifth position. Although it's not written in the music, make sure that you barre your third finger on the 2nd, 3rd, and 4th strings when playing the D chord in the third beat of the first measure, and barre your first finger on the same strings at the fourth beat of the first measure. The second lick (Fig. 6) also works over A7 and is based on a three-note melodic sequence. The last phrase, Fig. 7 (also over A7) is a position changing lick that starts on your first finger in eighth position and ends in third position.

Scales for "Metric"

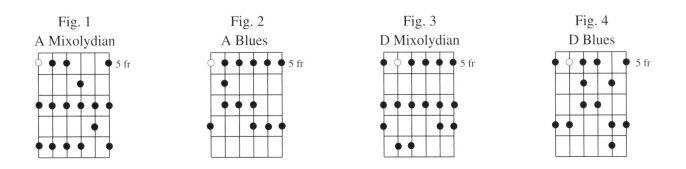

Fig. 1	Fig. 2	Fig. 3	Fig. 4
A Mixolydian	A Blues	D Mixolydian	D Blues

Samples Licks for "Metric"

Fig. 5

Fig. 6

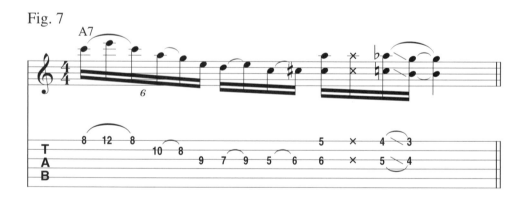

Fig. 7

FRIED EGGS

"Fried Eggs" is the most energetic and challenging of all the pieces in this book. The two *E blues scales* in Figs. 1 and 2 should be used against the verse and bridge while the two *B♭ blues* scales (Figs. 3 and 4) work over the chorus. To make it easier for you to switch scales, I have written Figs. 1 and 3 in roughly the same position. The same is true for Figs. 2 and 4. This will help you keep your ideas flowing between the verse and bridge and vice versa.

Initially you may find it difficult to phrase over this tune because of its fast tempo. Instead of trying to play a non-stop barrage of sixteenth notes, try a more rhythmic approach. Use more space, rhythmic sequences and held notes to build your solo. Then, when you do play a fast line, it will be much more dramatic and effective for the listener.

Perhaps even more of a challenge than soloing at this tempo is playing rhythm. Locking in tight with the bass and drums for a long period of time is in many ways the most difficult aspect of playing funk. This skill should be the primary goal of every guitar player, especially since playing rhythm is what you'll be doing at least 95% of the time! The sample rhythm part in Fig. 5 contains a chord voicing which is used frequently in this style. It's the chord that you slide into on the first beat. In the context of this exercise, it's an E13♯9 chord without the root. You can use this chord to create your own rhythm parts or just embellish the part shown in Fig. 5. Fig. 6 begins by outlining the E13♯9, then finishing with an E blues lick. The last example works over the chorus and primarily uses the B♭ blues scale in Fig. 4. Note the grace note slide from D♯ to E at the end of the second beat.

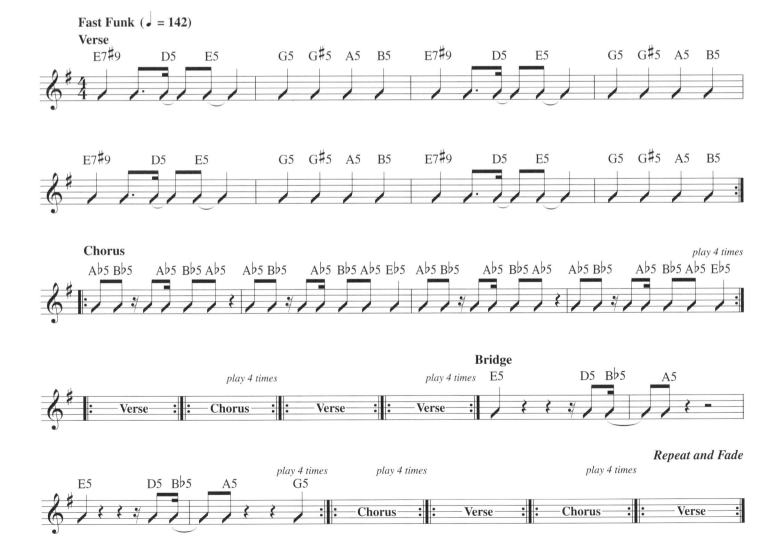

Scales for "Fried Eggs"

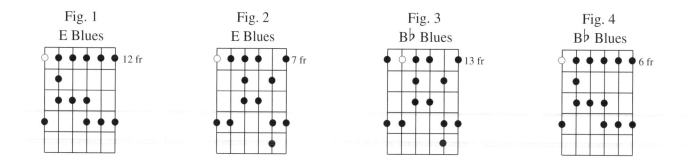

Samples Licks for "Fried Eggs"

Fig. 5

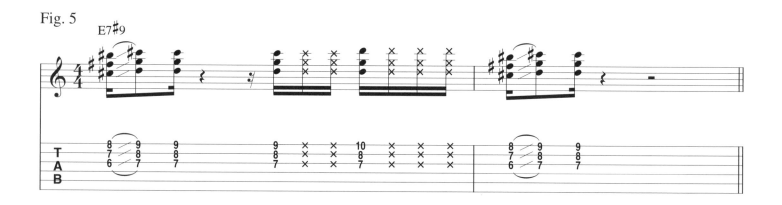

Fig. 6

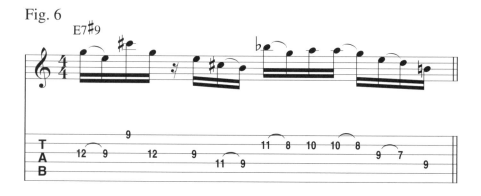

Fig. 7

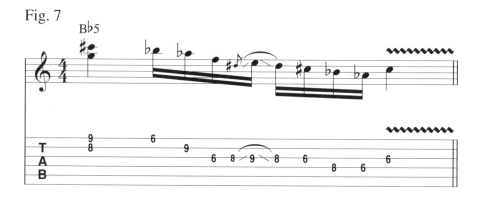

ᴀɴᴛɪᴍᴀᴛᴛᴇʀ

This tune's feel is inspired by a John Scofield recording. All of his albums recorded between 1984 and 1989 are brilliant examples of great funk ensemble playing. The chorus section of this chart is built around a repeating ii-V progression in C major, make *D Dorian* (Fig. 1) the primary scale choice for improvising. You may also use Fig. 2 (*D minor pentatonic*). During the bridge, the harmony switches to a static Fm7 chord. For this section, use Fig. 3 (*F minor pentatonic*) and Fig. 4 (*F Dorian*). Since the interlude returns to an implied D Dorian tonality, it should be treated the same way as the verse, using Figures 1 and 2.

The feel of this exercise could be described as a "half-time funk shuffle." It's the slowest of all the tunes in this chapter, so there may be a tendency to rush the tempo when improvising. Try to lay back and let the music pull you forward.

Most of the rhythm guitar phrases in this chapter are two measure repeated motifs usually involving double-stops, single notes and muted strings. All of these are common stylistic elements of funk guitar playing and it's important for you to be aware of this when developing your own guitar parts in this idiom. Study the first phrase (Fig. 5) to see how you can incorporate all these different elements. The second phrase (Fig. 6) is a bluesy idea that contains an "over-bend" or a bend greater than a whole step. The last lick (Fig.7) is interesting harmonically, and challenging from a technical standpoint. The second beat is made up of three notes "inside" the chord and three notes "outside" the chord. This kind of structure helps build tension and excitement in the phrase.

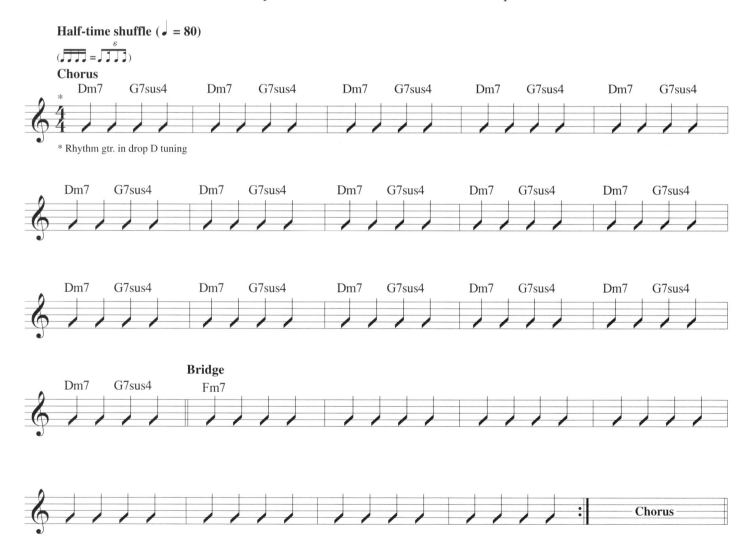

Half-time shuffle (♩ = 80)

Chorus

* Rhythm gtr. in drop D tuning

Bridge

Interlude

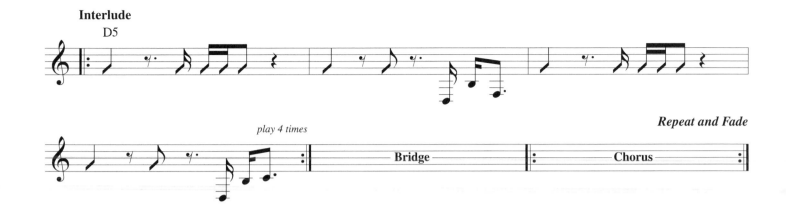

play 4 times

Repeat and Fade

Bridge

Chorus

Scales for "Antimatter"

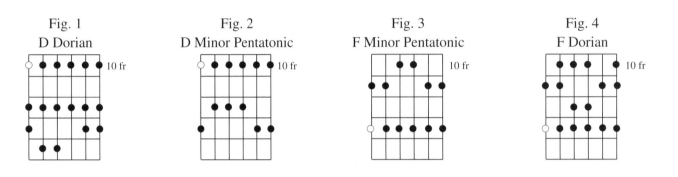

Fig. 1	Fig. 2	Fig. 3	Fig. 4
D Dorian	D Minor Pentatonic	F Minor Pentatonic	F Dorian

Samples Licks for "Antimatter"

Fig. 5

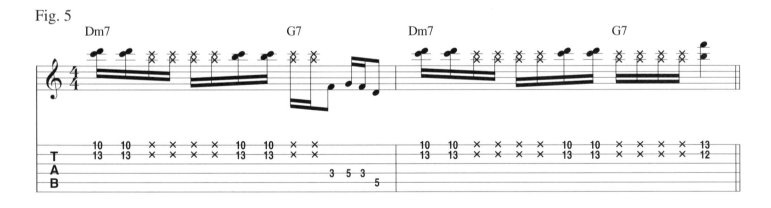

Fig. 6

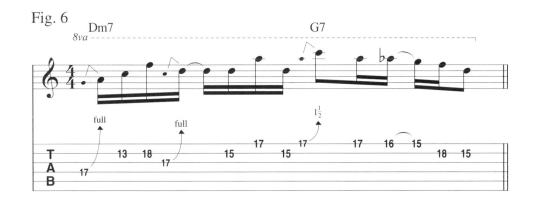

Fig. 7

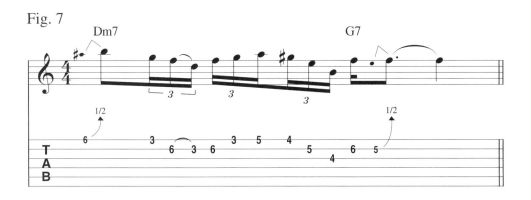

REBOUND

The form of this chart is divided into three parts. The verse is clearly in *B Mixolydian* (Fig. 1) and the chorus is in *E Mixolydian* (Fig. 4). Since the bridge is somewhat ambiguous, a good choice is the *B blues* scale in Fig. 2. Fig. 3, E *dominant pentatonic*, is an alternate choice for improvising over the chorus. One attribute of a good improviser is the ability to switch scales in the middle of a phrase without stopping the creative flow. Practice soloing from the verse to the chorus without stopping your line. This will help you to stop thinking about scales and allow you to focus on the direction and composition of your ideas.

The feel of this exercise is a standard hip hop beat. All sixteenth notes beamed in groups of four such as those in the sample licks should be interpreted as "swing" sixteenths. This means you should not play them evenly, but rather with a "long-short-long-short" feeling.

Fig. 5 is comprised mostly of single notes and represents a type of rhythm guitar style frequently used in funk. This is similar to the non-chordal rhythm parts found in rock, and shows that chords are not the only elements used in rhythm playing. The next phrase (Fig. 6) should be used against the verse and is a great example of a melodic sequence. The repeating pattern in this lick is a four-note motif, which starts on a chromatic note and is then followed by three diatonic notes. Try creating your own sequence with this pattern. Fig. 7 works over the chorus and is fairly tricky from a technical standpoint. It will be easier if you begin this phrase on your second finger. There is also a difficult stretch on the second-to-last note of this lick.

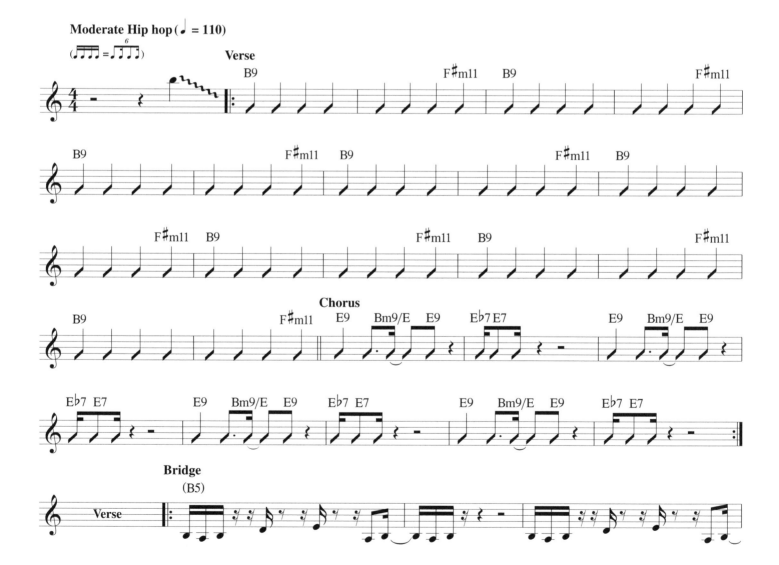

Repeat and Fade

Chorus | Verse

Scales for "Rebound"

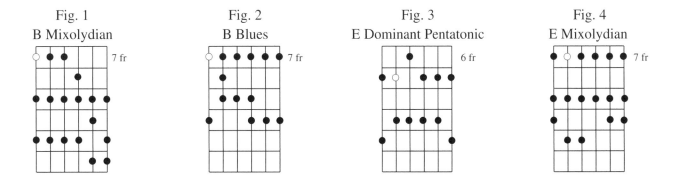

Fig. 1	Fig. 2	Fig. 3	Fig. 4
B Mixolydian	B Blues	E Dominant Pentatonic	E Mixolydian

Samples Licks for "Rebound"

Fig. 5

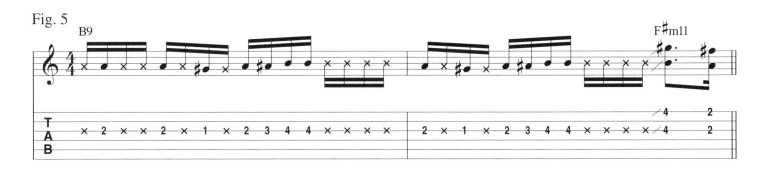

Fig. 6

Fig. 7

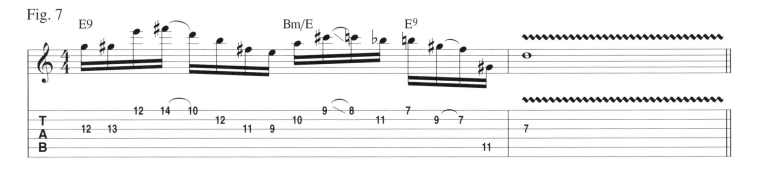

SUBURBAN JUNGLE

With the exception of a sixteen bar bridge in G Dorian, this entire chart is composed from a two measure repeated motif in G minor (Aeolian). The *G Aeolian* scales in Figs. 1 and 2 work over the chorus while Fig. 5 (*G Dorian*) works over the bridge. The scales in Figs. 3 and 4 sound good over any part of the progression. The only difference between G Aeolian and G Dorian is the sixth note, which is Eb for G Aeolian and E natural for G Dorian. At times you'll hear different parts coming in and out of the mix, but this has no effect on the harmony of the tune.

The rhythms in this exercise are based on slow, even sixteenth notes. Your main concern as a soloist or rhythm player is to avoid rushing the tempo. Try to lay behind or ideally *center* your feel as much as possible. Since the audio was created with a sequencer, the feel is 100% even and perfect, which can feel a bit awkward if you're not used to playing with a drum machine or metronome.

All the sample licks for this tune follow the main chord progression in G minor. Fig. 6 is a harmonized rhythm line typical of guitar parts used in late '70s funk tunes. It's important to keep your picking hand moving down and up in sync with the underlying sixteenth-note pulse while your fretting hand alternates between playing notes and muting. The next lick (Fig. 7) can be used over the chorus and is played in tenth position starting on your first finger. The final phrase (Fig. 8) offers a jazzy sound and clearly outlines the chord changes. The hammer-on and pull-off markings for all the licks are optional. Use your own judgment when it comes to articulation.

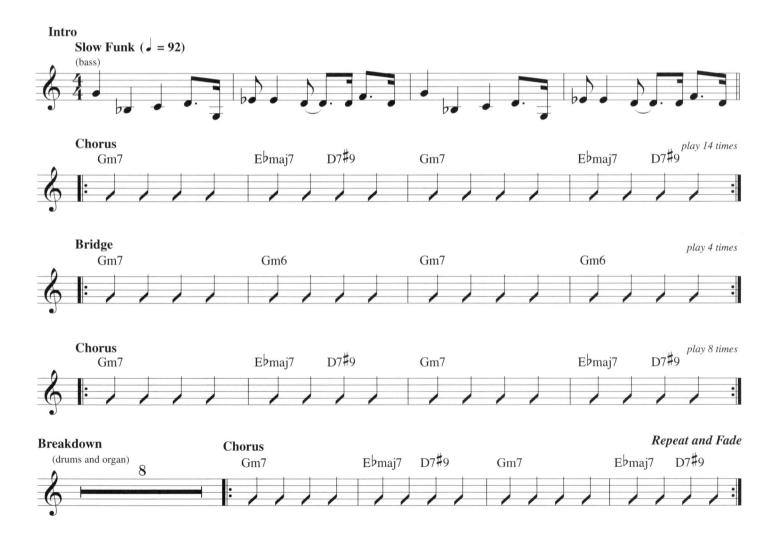

Scales for "Suburban Jungle"

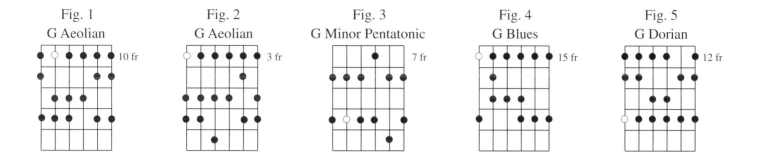

Samples Licks for "Suburban Jungle"

Fig. 6

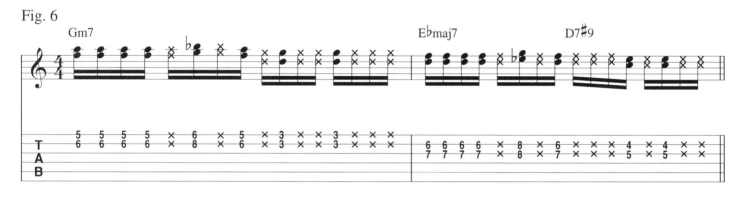

Fig. 7

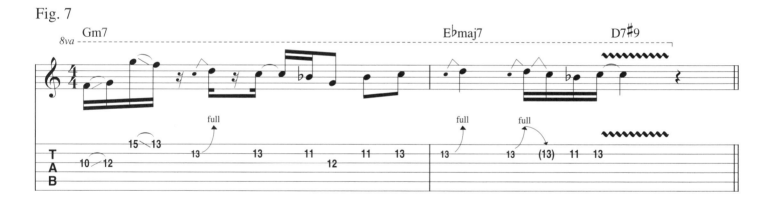

Fig. 8

LATE NITE

"Late Nite is an example of a funk shuffle. The verse is based around the *G Mixolydian* scale (Fig. 1) while the chorus is based on *G Dorian* (Fig. 2). For the pre-chorus, use the *E minor pentatonic* scale (Fig.3) over the first two measures and then switch to the G Dorian scale for the rest of the section. During the bridge you must change scales again. Start the first two measures of the bridge with Fig. 2 (G Dorian), then switch to Fig. 4 (*E♭ Mixolydian*) for the third measure and back again to Fig. 2 for the fourth measure. Repeat these steps for measures 5-9 of the bridge. As a much simpler option, the *G blues* scale in Fig. 5 can essentially be used over any part of the tune.

Normally shuffles are not put in the category of funk, but rather blues or rock. However, by using slap bass and other funk instrumentation (such as a clavinet or wah-pedal) a shuffle can become funky. Accenting every *even-numbered* eighth note in a 12/8 shuffle is another way to enhance a shuffle's funkiness.

All of the sample licks for "Late Nite" are designed to work over the verse section or G7 chord. The first lick, Fig. 6, is a four-bar rhythm guitar idea that utilizes double-stops and left hand muting. Fig. 7 is a cool position changing blues lick. Remember to play the second-to-last note of the first measure (F) with your first finger. The last phrase, Fig. 8, is another rhythm guitar idea. Make sure that you don't pick the notes you're sliding into. Also watch your intonation on the double bend at the end of the phrase.

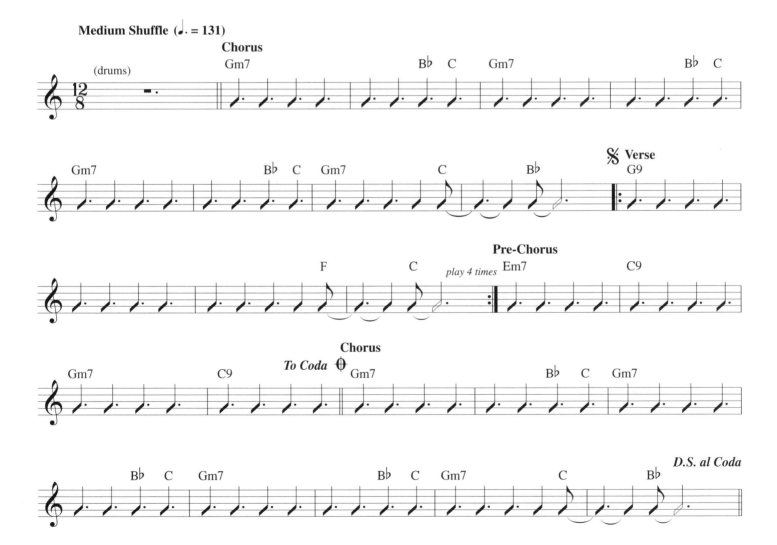

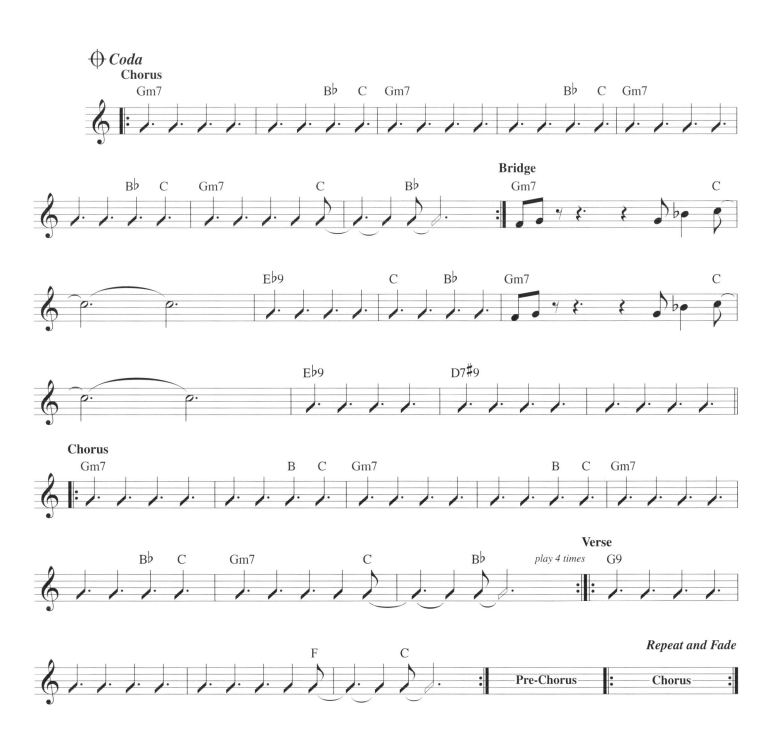

Scales for "Late Nite"

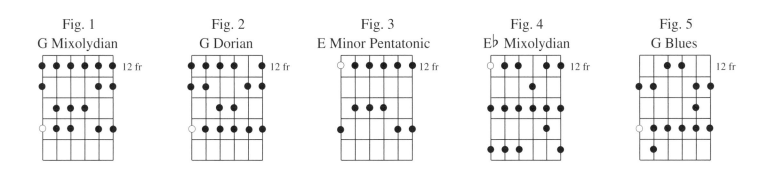

Fig. 1	Fig. 2	Fig. 3	Fig. 4	Fig. 5
G Mixolydian	G Dorian	E Minor Pentatonic	E♭ Mixolydian	G Blues

Samples Licks for "Late Nite"

Fig. 6

Fig. 7

Fig. 8

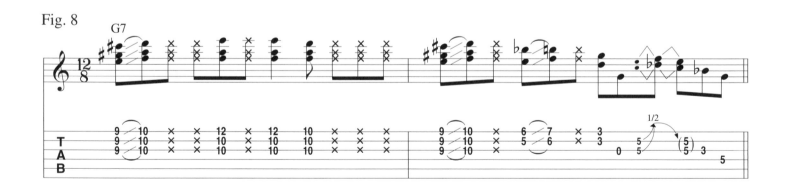

Makeover

"Makeover" is made up of three sections. Each is in a different key and must therefore be approached with a different scale. Because of this, I have written all the scale fingerings in the same area of the fingerboard. This makes it easier to switch from one scale to the next. Fig. 1 (*E blues*) is for improvising over the verse and Fig. 2 (*A Mixolydian*) is for the chorus. Over the bridge you should begin with Fig. 3 (*F♯ minor pentatonic*) against the F♯7♯9 chord, then switch to Fig. 2 for the A7 chord. When you get the C♯7 chord, switch to Fig. 4 (*C♯ minor pentatonic*). As an option, you can use Fig. 3 over the chorus as well as over the A7 chord in the bridge.

The sparseness of the verse section is contrasted by the more active chorus and bridge. Try to utilize this element in your approach to improvising. Make an obvious change in the density of your phrases when going from one section to another. This will enhance and develop your ideas and provide better dynamics overall.

The sample rhythm phrase in Fig. 5 is comprised mainly of major sixth intervals. Intervals are useful in creating funk rhythm parts because they are lighter and easier to move around than chords, but fuller sounding than single notes. In the next phrase (Fig. 6) you must bend the D note on the 15th fret up a whole step to E and hold it while playing G on the high E string. Be sure not to let the bend slip when you go to play the G. The last lick (Fig. 7) works over the F♯7♯9 chord in the bridge. It is composed entirely of notes from the F♯ minor pentatonic scale and contains some wide stretches, string skipping and position changes.

Scales for "Makeover"

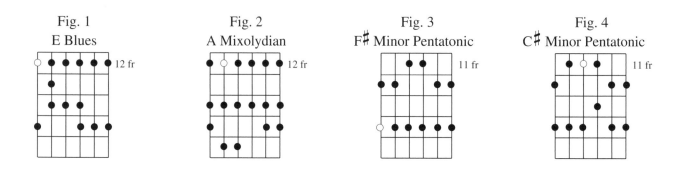

Fig. 1
E Blues

Fig. 2
A Mixolydian

Fig. 3
F♯ Minor Pentatonic

Fig. 4
C♯ Minor Pentatonic

Fig. 5

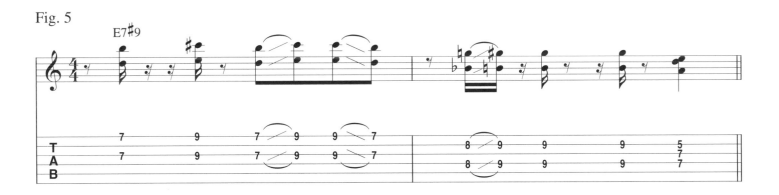

Fig. 6

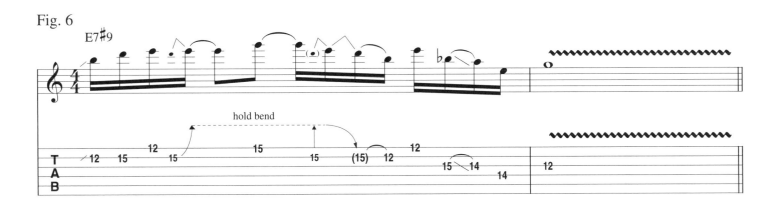

Fig. 7

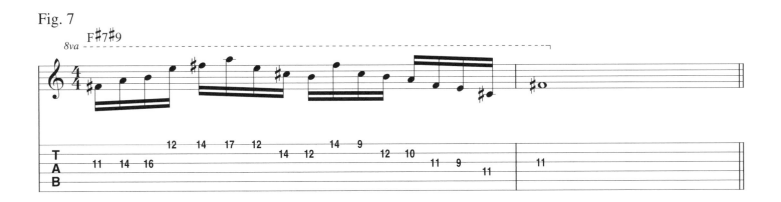

CHAPTER 4: JAZZ JAMS
INTRODUCTION TO JAZZ GUITAR

A teacher of mine once told me, "If you can play jazz you can play anything!" Whether you agree with this or not, there's no question that jazz is one of the most fascinating, challanging and timeless styles of music. To play it you must have a thorough understanding of music theory and how to apply it on your instrument, as well as a good sense of melody and the ability to listen and react quickly and effectively to what others are playing. It is also important (as it is with any style) to be familiar with the musical traditions, repetoire, history and defining attributes of the genre. Only by aquiring these skills and essential knowledge can you become a good jazz musician.

One of the most prominant features of jazz is the emphasis on improvisation. The ability to create interesting and emotionally-moving melodic, harmonic and rhythmic statements within a musical framework is the main criteria by which jazz musicians are judged. The best way to develop this skill is to practice improvising over a variety of different jazz styles and feels such as swing, latin, waltz, bebop, blues, modal, etc., and to learn all the necessary scales, arpeggios and phrases you need to construct your ideas from.

IMPORTANT INFORMATION

1. Alternate Chord Changes – Any chord names written in parenthesis should be considered alternates or substitutes. This means they may occur now and then, but not at any preordained time. You may also address them at any time during improvisation without the risk of clashing.

2. Coda Sections – Most of the tracks in this chapter have a repeating form which on the last time jumps to a coda section for the end. Remember, this coda section is *not part of* the main repeating form.

3. Scale Fingering Proximity – The suggested scales given for each exercise are generally written in the same area of the fingerboard. This allows you to switch from one scale to another more easily, however it does not mean you can not use the entire fingerboard when improvising.

You Are All the Things

The first track, "You Are All the Things," has a 36-bar form based primarily around the key of Ab major beginning on the vi chord, Fm7. The order of modulations and the appropriate scale choices are as follows:

> Meas. 1-5 (Ab major) use Fig. 1, *F Aeolian*
>
> Meas. 6-8 (C major) use Fig. 2, *C major*
>
> Meas. 9-13 (Eb major) use Fig. 3, *C Aeolian*
>
> Meas. 14-20 (G major) use Fig. 4, *G major*
>
> Meas. 21-23 (E major) use Fig. 5, *E major*
>
> Meas. 24-29 (Ab major) use Fig. 1, *F Aeolian*
>
> Meas. 30 (Cb major) use Fig. 6, *Db Dorian*
>
> Meas. 31-36 (Ab major) use Fig. 1, *F Aeolian*

Over the 7-bar Coda section, use *F Aeolian* for the first six measures, and *C Aeolian* for the final measure.

As I stated in the introduction, these are only suggested scales. There are many other scale choices you could use against this chart. It's also important for you to practice approaching each chord *separately* as opposed to grouping them within one key. This will make your ideas much more expressive. Although it's important in jazz to outline the chords and key centers, don't feel that you must address every chord all the time. It's much better to let a few chords go by and prepare yourself for a later chord rather than trying to nail all of them.

Perhaps the most important thing to keep in mind is to try to play *"through the changes"* as opposed to *"on the changes."* Playing "through the changes" means to start an idea in one key and seamlessly continue it (without stopping) through to the next key. This is done by only changing the notes that need to be changed in order to fit the new key. The phrases in Figs. 7-9 are good examples of how to play through the changes at different points in the progression. Fig. 7 works over measures 5-7 going from the key of Ab to the key of C. Fig. 8 works over measures 13-15 (key of Eb, to the key of G) and Fig. 9 works over measures 29-31 (key of Ab, to the key of Cb, to the key of Ab).

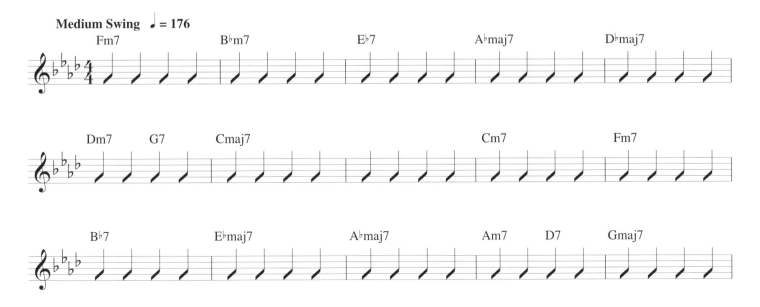

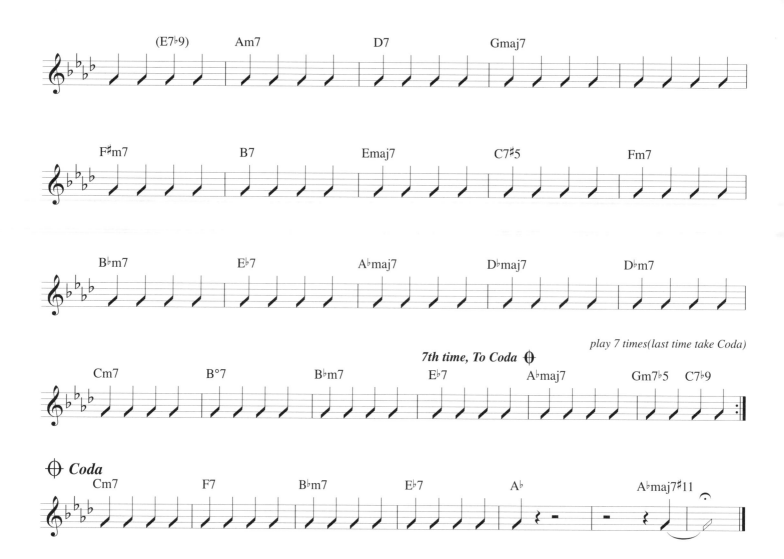

Scales for "You Are All the Things"

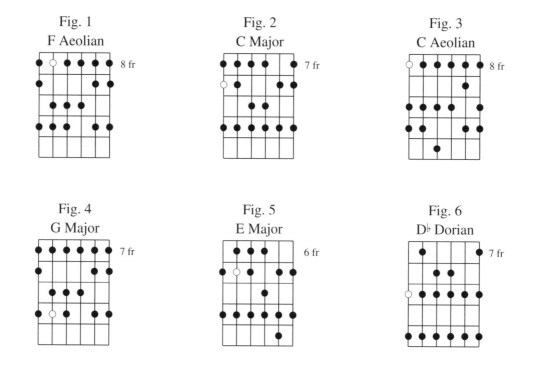

Sample Licks for "You Are All the Things

Fig. 7

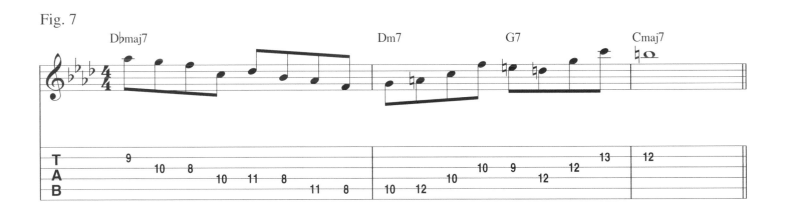

Fig. 8

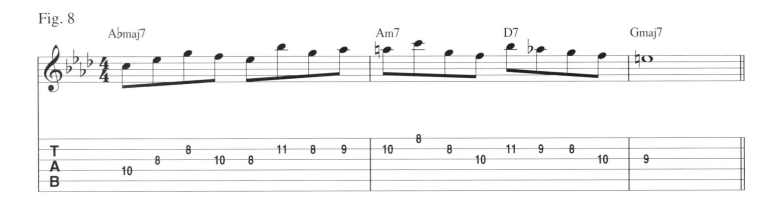

Fig. 9

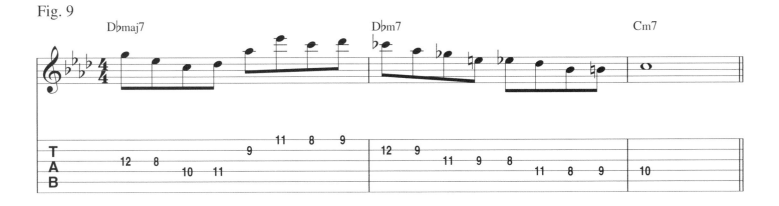

BLOOZE IN EFF

"Blooze in Eff" is a standard 12-bar jazz/blues in the key of F. The common chord changes are written above while the alternate or substitute changes appear in parentheses. The alternate set may be used occasionally to vary and build the harmonic flavor of the tune.

The letters "alt." after the C7 chord in the tenth measure stand for the word "altered." This means the C7 chord includes a raised or lowered 5th (G♯ or G♭) and/or a raised or lowered 9th (D♯ or D♭).

The primary scale for this chart is Fig. 1, *F blues*. It can be used effectively over the entire exercise, although it would not be "stylistically correct" to use Fig. 1 exclusively. The other scales in Figs. 2-6 will help you address each chord and key center in a specific manner. Fig. 2, *B♭ Mixolydian*, can be used over any B♭7 chord. The *B diminished 7 arpeggio* shown in Fig. 3 sounds good over beats three and four of the second measure as well as the entire sixth measure. Fig. 4, *D Super Locrian*, works great over any D7 chord while Fig. 5, *G Dorian*, is an alternative scale for measures 8-12. Finally, the *C Super Locrian* scale shown in Fig. 6 works perfectly over C7 and C7alt.

To help you bring new sounds into your playing, select a portion of the chart you wish to add a new scale to. For example, try improvising over the entire progression using just the F blues scale (Fig. 1). When you get to the ninth and tenth bars, Gm7 to C7alt., use Fig. 5 (G Dorian) for Gm7 and Fig. 6 (C Super Locrian) for C7alt. These will be the only two measures you'll have to worry about changing scales. By not overwhelming yourself with too much information, you'll allow yourself to prepare your ideas better and make a smoother transition from one scale to the next. Once you feel comfortable with this, try doing it over another part of the progresssion with a different scale.

The first sample phrase (Fig. 7) works over bars 5-7. Notice the way the line moves from one scale to the next in a smooth and natural fashion. The next phrase, Fig. 8, is useful over the fourth and fifth measures, and applies the F Super Locrian scale (not shown) over the F7 chord. To find this scale, take Fig. 4 (D Super Locrian) and change the fret number "4" to "7." This will transpose the scale to F. The last phrase (Fig. 9) works over bars 9-11 and uses superimposed triad arpeggios (A major and G♭ major) against the C7alt. chord.

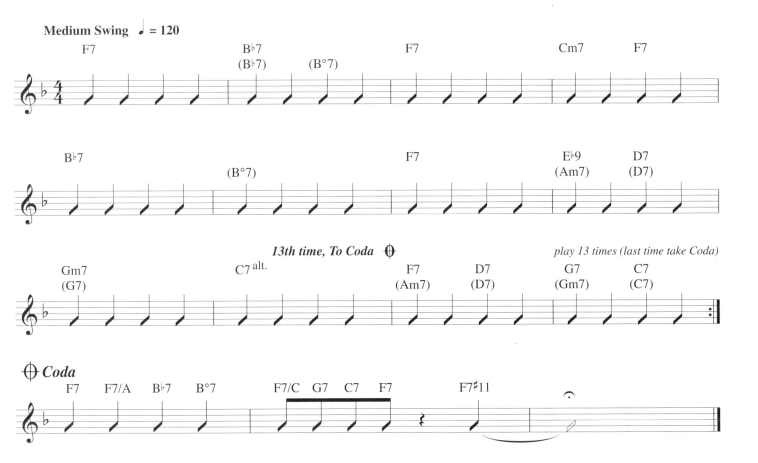

Scales for "Blooze in Eff"

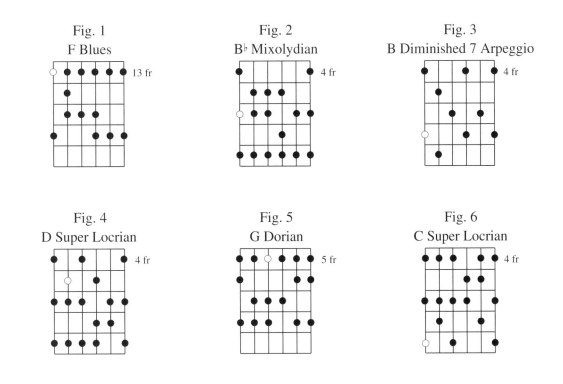

Fig. 1
F Blues
13 fr

Fig. 2
B♭ Mixolydian
4 fr

Fig. 3
B Diminished 7 Arpeggio
4 fr

Fig. 4
D Super Locrian
4 fr

Fig. 5
G Dorian
5 fr

Fig. 6
C Super Locrian
4 fr

Sample Licks for "Blooze in Eff"

Fig. 7

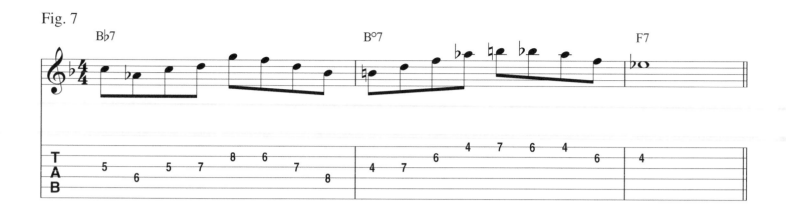

Fig. 8

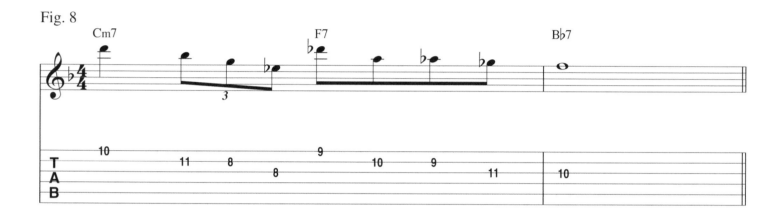

Fig. 9

MY PRINTS WILL COME SOMEDAY

This tune is an example of a jazz waltz. The defining characteristic of any waltz is a 3/4 time signature, however a *jazz* waltz differs from other waltz styles in the way the beats are felt. Normally songs in 3/4 time have a "quarter-note feel" with an emphasis (or accent) on the first beat. In a jazz waltz the accents are on the first beat as well as the "and" after beat two. Another way to interpret this is to think of the accents falling on every dotted quarter-note.

The main key center for this tune is B♭ major. The order of modulations and appropriate scale choices are as follows:

> Meas. 1-3 (B♭ major) use Figs. 1 or 3, *B♭ major*
>
> Meas. 4-6 (C minor) use Fig. 5, *E♭ major*
>
> Meas. 7-19 (B♭ major) use Figs. 1 or 3, *B♭ major*
>
> Meas. 20-22 (C minor) use Fig. 5, *E♭ major*
>
> Meas. 23-24 (B♭ major) use Figs. 1 or 3, *B♭ major*
>
> Meas. 25-27 (E♭ major) use Fig. 5, *E♭ major*
>
> Meas. 28 use Fig. 4, *C♯ diminished arpeggio*
>
> Meas. 29-36 (B♭ major) use Figs. 1 or 3, *B♭ major*

Figures two, four and six are not essential to this exercise, but if used properly will add a tremendous amount of color and excitment to your lines. They are useful for addressing specific chords within the progression. Fig. 2, *G Spanish Phrygian*, is a great choice for all the G7 chords, while Fig. 6, *F Super Locrian*, is good for all the F7 chords. Fig. 4 works well for any C♯ or E diminished 7th chords. Try experimenting with these sounds a little at a time to get your ear used to them. It may be challanging at first, but it's subtle elements like these which give jazz its unique sound and flavor.

The first sample lick (Fig. 7) works over measures 9-12 and 13-16. Notice the sequential pattern of the first two measures. Repeating the general shape of a melodic line is an effective way to develop an idea. Fig. 8 should be played over measures 25-29 while Fig. 9 works well for measures 1-5 and 17-21.

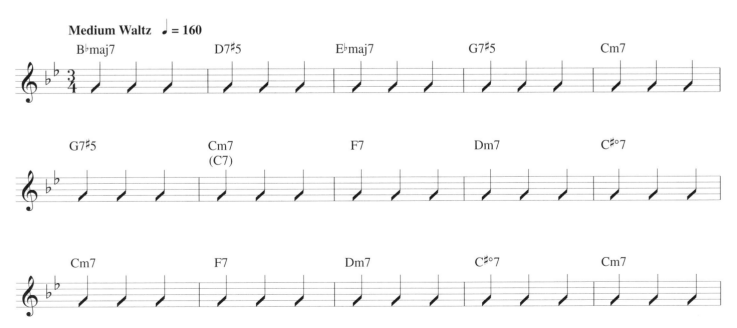

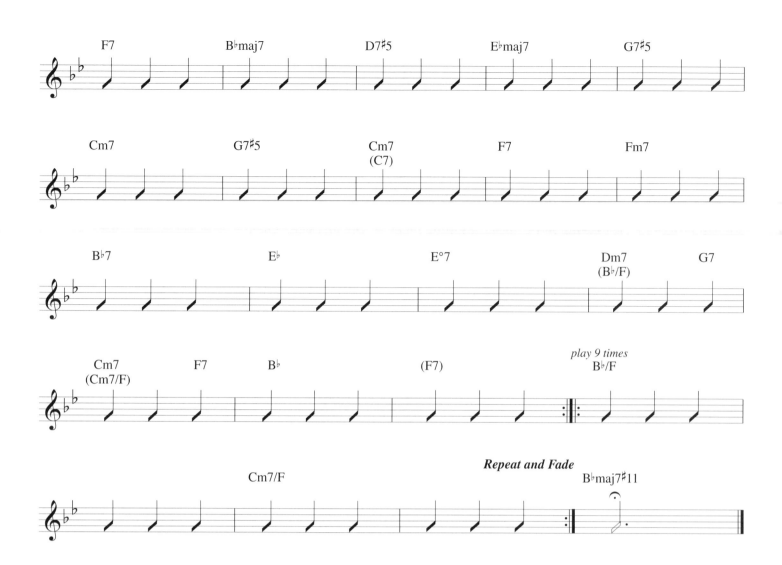

Scales for "My Prints Will Come Someday"

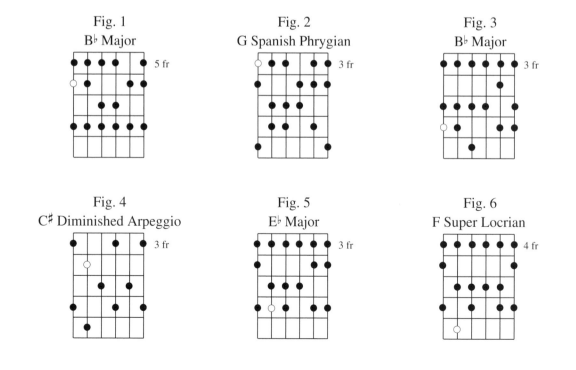

Fig. 1
B♭ Major
5 fr

Fig. 2
G Spanish Phrygian
3 fr

Fig. 3
B♭ Major
3 fr

Fig. 4
C♯ Diminished Arpeggio
3 fr

Fig. 5
E♭ Major
3 fr

Fig. 6
F Super Locrian
4 fr

Sample Licks for "My Prints Will Come Someday"

Fig. 7

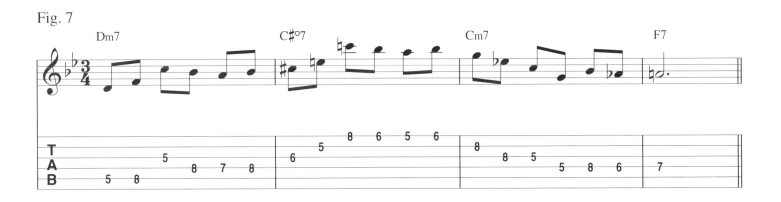

Fig. 8

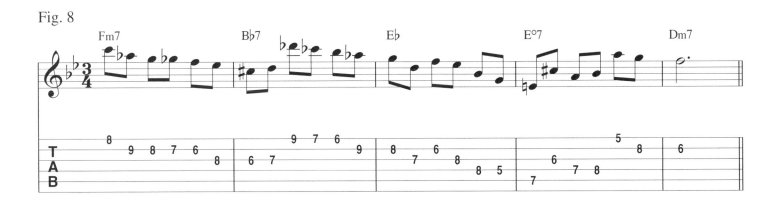

Fig. 9

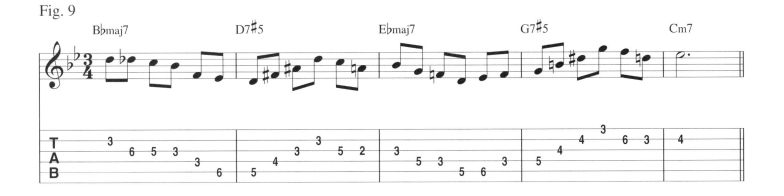

⦿ DOLPHINS ON GREEN ST.

"Dolphins on Green St." is a 32-bar progression in the key of C major. One of the more interesting aspects of this track is the way it alternates rhythmically between "Latin" and "swing" feels. Eighth-notes played with a Latin feel are "straight" or even, rather than "swung." The modulations and suggested scale choices are as follows:

Meas. 1-2 (C major) use Fig. 1, *C major*

Meas. 3-4 (B♭ major) use Fig. 2, *C Dorian*

Meas. 5 (G major) use Fig. 3, *C Lydian*

Meas. 6 (G♭ major) use Fig. 4, *G Super Locrian*

Meas. 7-12 (C major) use Fig. 1, *C major*

Meas. 13-15 (E♭ major) use Fig. 5, *E♭ major*

Meas. 16-18 (C major) use Fig. 1, *C major*

Meas. 19-20 (B♭ major) use Fig. 2, *C Dorian*

Meas. 21 (G major) use Fig. 3, *C Lydian*

Meas. 22 (G♭ major) use Fig. 4, *G Super Locrian*

Meas. 23-25 (C major) use Fig. 1, *C major*

Meas. 26-27 (A minor) use Fig. 6, *A harmonic minor*

Meas. 28 (E minor) use Fig. 3, *C Lydian*

Meas. 29-32 (C major) use Fig. 1, *C major*

Over the 6-bar Coda section, use *C major* for the first four measures, *D Lydian* (Fig. 3 up a half-step) for the next measure and *C Lydian* for the final measure.

Some of the scales shown in Figures 1-6 may be transposed and used in other parts of the progression. For example by changing the fret number of Fig. 4 (G Super Locrian) from a 7 to a 10, you can now use the scale over the B♭7 in measure 14. Another useful transposition is to lower the fingering in Fig. 3 (C Lydian) by one halfstep and use it over the D♭7 chord in measure 6.

The sample licks in Figs. 7-9 are all models of how to improvise "through" chord changes as opposed to "on" the changes. Notice how the melodic ideas flow and develop smoothly from chord to chord without any awkward or unnatural leaps and pauses. Fig. 7 is designed to work over measures 5-7, Fig. 8 over measures 25-28 and Fig. 9 over measures 15-17. The sequential phrasing in Fig. 9 is a particularly effective element in moving from the key of E♭ to the key of C.

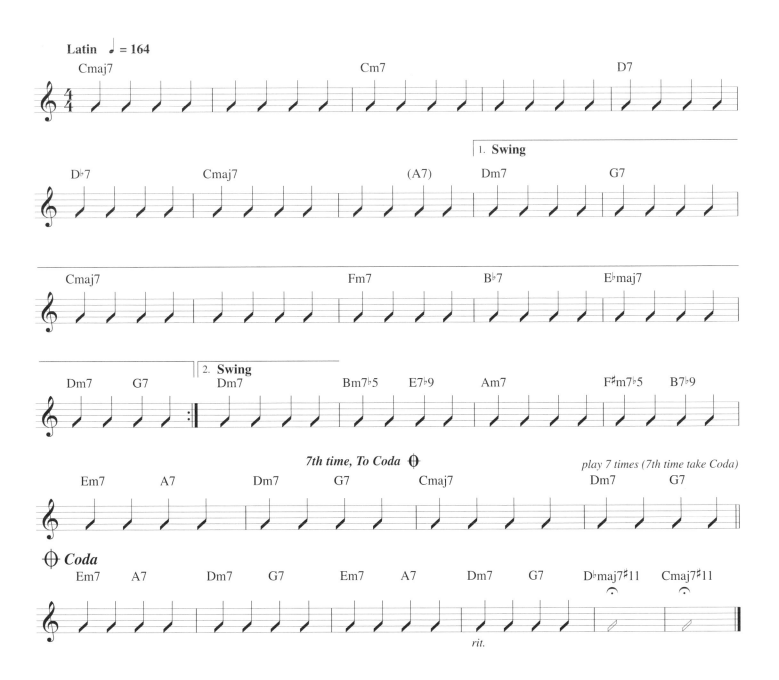

Scales for "Dolphins on Green St."

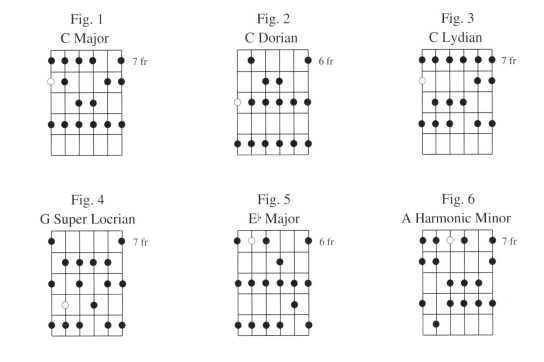

Fig. 1
C Major

Fig. 2
C Dorian

Fig. 3
C Lydian

Fig. 4
G Super Locrian

Fig. 5
E♭ Major

Fig. 6
A Harmonic Minor

Sample Licks for "Dolphins on Green St."

Fig. 7

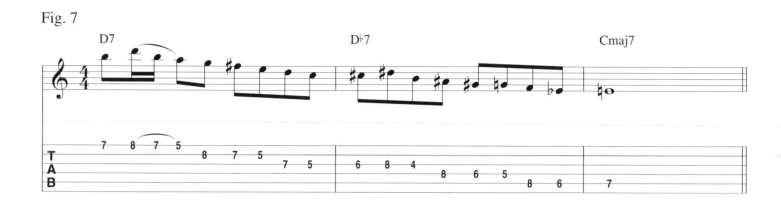

Fig. 8

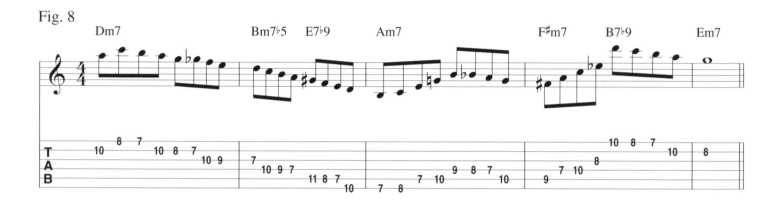

Fig. 9

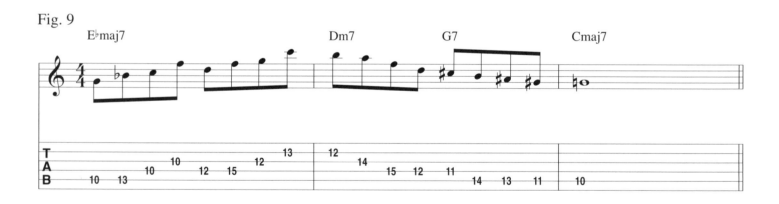

IMPERSONATIONS

"Impersonations" is an example of a "modal" jazz composition. Although it has the fastest tempo of all the tracks in this chapter, it's the least complicated harmonically. In fact it has only two chords; Dm7 and E♭m7. The entire form is: sixteen bars of Dm7, eight bars of E♭m7, and then eight bars of Dm7. Over the Dm7 chords you may use Figs. 1-3, while over the E♭m7 chords use Figs. 4-6.

The main challange of this tune is not to navigate through the changes, but rather to improvise as creatively as possible given the limited harmonic material. One way that you can create more interesting melodic lines is to play "outside" of the given chords. To do this effectively, try to start an idea "inside" the key, continue it "outside" the key and finally resolve the line on a chord tone. A simple way to quickly find notes that are outside of the key you're in is to take whichever inside scale you're playing and move it up or down by one half step. This will allow you to keep your creative flow without having to think too hard about finding the "good" notes versus the "bad."

All of the sample phrases for this chart demonstrate how to switch from one scale to the other. Fig. 7 contains a four note melodic sequence and should be played over measures 15-17. Fig. 8 is a descending line that works over bars 23-25, and Fig. 9 is a wide-interval phrase that moves from Dm7 to E♭m7.

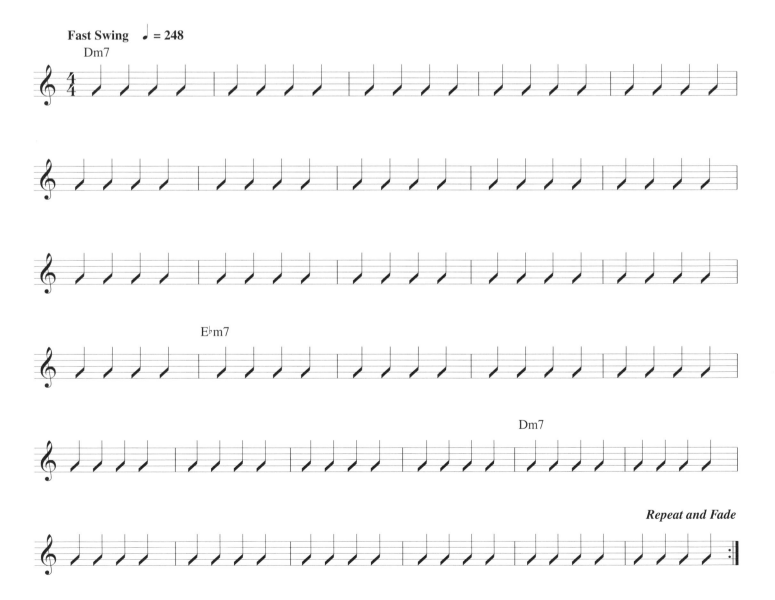

Scales for "Impersonations"

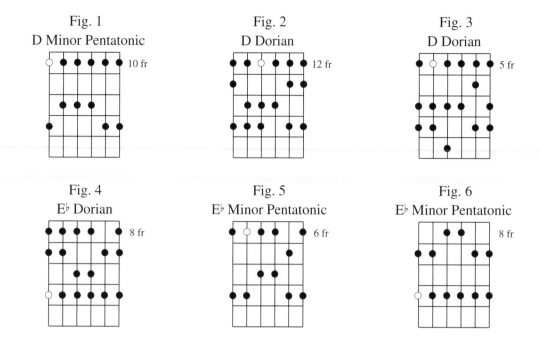

Fig. 1
D Minor Pentatonic
10 fr

Fig. 2
D Dorian
12 fr

Fig. 3
D Dorian
5 fr

Fig. 4
E♭ Dorian
8 fr

Fig. 5
E♭ Minor Pentatonic
6 fr

Fig. 6
E♭ Minor Pentatonic
8 fr

Sample Licks for "Impersonations"

Fig. 7

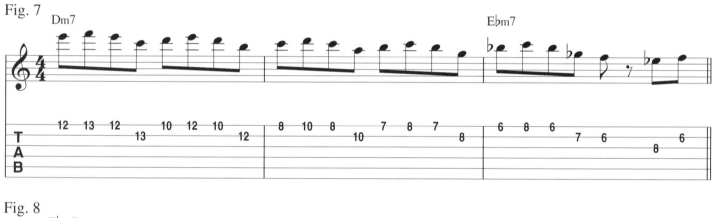

Fig. 8

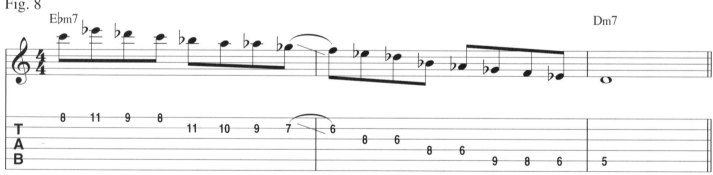

Fig. 9

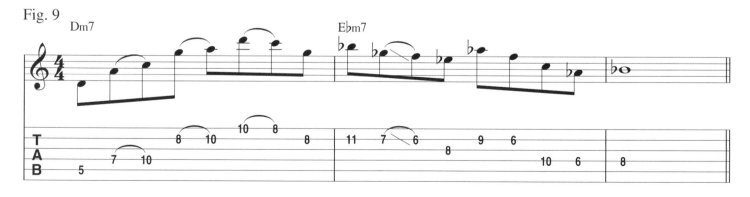

BOBBY AND SAL

"Bobby and Sal" is the exact opposite of the previous tune. It's the slowest of all the tunes, yet the most harmonically complex. Because of its slow tempo, the form is only played three times and key changes occur frequently, sometimes within a measure. Here are the key centers and appropriate scales for this chart:

A Section
Meas. 1, beats 1 and 2 (D♭ major) use Fig. 1, *E♭ Dorian*

Meas. 1, beats 3 and 4 (E♭ minor) use Fig. 2, *B♭ Super Locrian*

Meas. 2 (D♭ major) use Fig. 1, *E♭ Dorian*

Meas. 3, beats 1 and 2 (D♭ major) use Fig. 1, *E♭ Dorian*

Meas. 3, beats 3 and 4 use Fig. 3, *G♭ Mixolydian #4*

Meas. 4-6 (D♭ major) use Fig. 1, *E♭ Dorian*

Meas. 7, beats 1 and 2 (A♭ major) use Fig. 5, *B♭ Dorian*

Meas. 7, beats 3 and 4 (D♭ major) use Fig. 1, *E♭ Dorian*

1st ending
Meas. 8, beats 1 and 2 (D♭ major) use Fig. 1, *E♭ Dorian*

Meas. 8, beats 3 and 4 (E♭ minor) use Fig. 2, *B♭ Super Locrian*

2nd ending
Meas. 9 , beats 1 and 2 (E♭ minor) use Fig. 1, *E♭ Dorian*

Meas. 9, beats 3 and 4 (D major) use Fig. 6, *E Dorian*

B Section
Meas. 10 (D major) use Fig. 6, *E Dorian*

Meas. 11, beats 1 and 2 (D major) use Fig. 6, *E Dorian*

Meas. 11, beats 3 and 4 (F major) use Fig. 7, *G Dorian*

Meas. 12-13 (D major) use Fig. 6, *E Dorian*

Meas. 14-16 (C major) use Fig. 8, *D Dorian*

Meas. 17, beat 1 (F major) use Fig. 7, *G Dorian*

Meas. 17, beat 2 (E major) use Fig. 9, *B Mixolydian*

Meas. 17, beats 3 and 4 (E♭ minor) use Fig. 2, *B♭ Super Locrian*

A Section
Meas. 18-25, same as meas. 1-8

Fig. 10 is an arpeggiated figure that works over the opening two bars of the progression. The second phrase (Fig. 11) utilizes a triplet feel and should be played over the seventh and/or twenty-fourth measure. Although Fig. 12 contains a few tricky fingerings, it sound great over bars sixteen and seventeen.

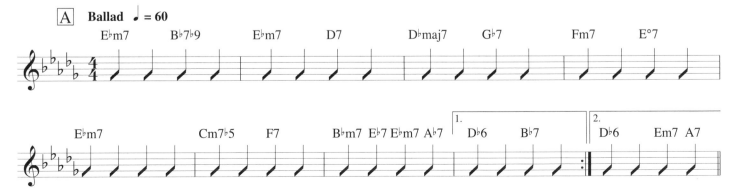

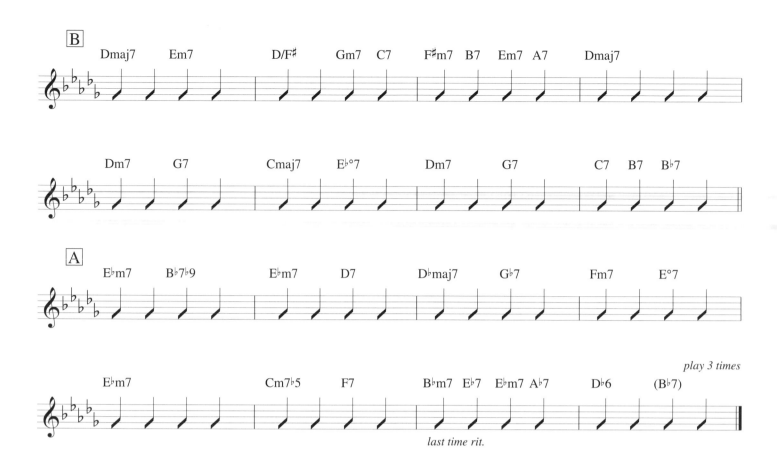

Scales for "Bobby and Sal"

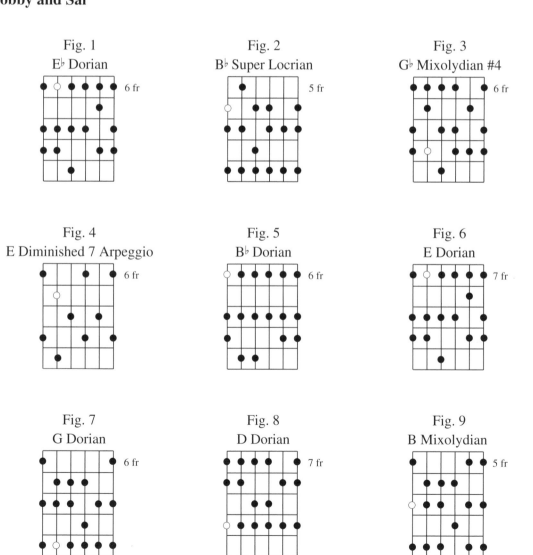

Fig. 1
Eb Dorian
6 fr

Fig. 2
Bb Super Locrian
5 fr

Fig. 3
Gb Mixolydian #4
6 fr

Fig. 4
E Diminished 7 Arpeggio
6 fr

Fig. 5
Bb Dorian
6 fr

Fig. 6
E Dorian
7 fr

Fig. 7
G Dorian
6 fr

Fig. 8
D Dorian
7 fr

Fig. 9
B Mixolydian
5 fr

Bobby and Sal

Sample Licks for "Bobby and Sal"

Fig. 10

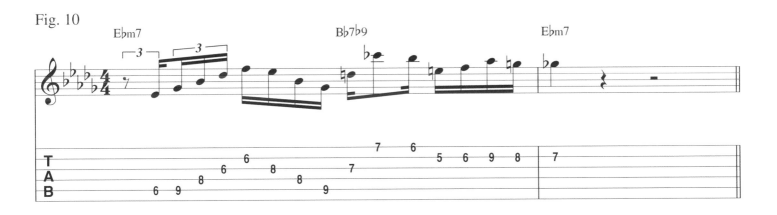

Fig. 11

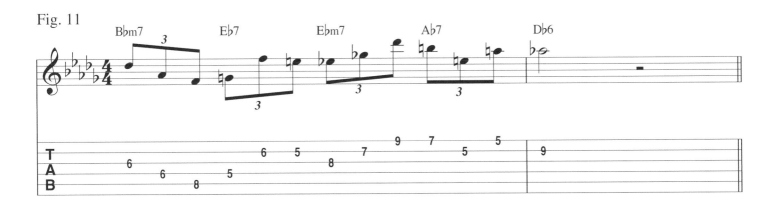

Fig. 12

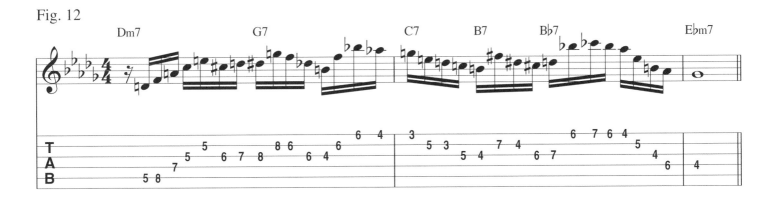

CONFISCATION

"Confiscation" is written in a style reminiscent of the great saxophonist Charlie Parker. He and trumpeter Dizzy Gillespie are credited with founding a style of jazz called *Bebop*. Bebop is characterized by fast tempos, complex harmony and busy chord progressions. Below are the key centers and suggested scales for this chart:

Meas. 1-3 (F major) use Fig. 1, *F Major*

Meas. 4 (Bb major) use Fig. 2, *C Dorian*

Meas. 5 (Eb major) use Fig. 3, *Bb Mixolydian*

Meas. 6 (G minor) use Fig. 4, *G Harmonic Minor*

Meas. 7 (C major) use Fig. 5, *G Mixolydian*

Meas. 8 (F minor) use Fig. 8, *C Super Locrian*

Meas. 9-11 (F major) use Fig. 1, *F Major*

Meas. 12 (Bb major) use Fig. 2, *C Dorian*

Meas. 13 (Eb major) use Fig. 3, *Bb Mixolydian*

Meas. 14 (G minor) use Fig. 4, *G Harmonic Minor*

Meas. 15-16 (F major) use Fig. 1, *F Major*

Meas. 17-20 (Bb major) use Fig. 6, *Bb Major*

Meas. 21-23 (Db major) use Fig. 7, *Db Major*

Meas. 24-27 (F major) use Fig. 1, *F Major*

Meas. 28 (Bb major) use Fig. 2, *C Dorian*

Meas. 29 (Eb major) use Fig. 3, *Bb Mixolydian*

Meas. 30 (G minor) use Fig. 4, *G Harmonic Minor*

Meas. 31-39 (F major) use Fig. 1, *F Major*

Meas. 40 (Db major) use Fig. 7, *Db Major*

One of the best ways to improve your ability to play over changes is to compose and write down phrases of your own which address problem areas in a particular tune. This will increase your soloing vocabulary and help you gain a clearer vision of what you ultimately want to play. Learning the sample phrases in this book is a good start and can serve as a model for creating your own ideas.

Looking at the sample licks, the first one (Fig. 9) demonstrates how to approach bars five through eight. Notice that the connecting interval between different chords is almost always a half step or whole step. This gives the line a more natural motion and continuous flow. Fig. 10 works against measures 23 through 25, and the last lick, Fig. 11, can be used over bars 1-4, 9-12 and 25-28.

Scales for "Confiscation"

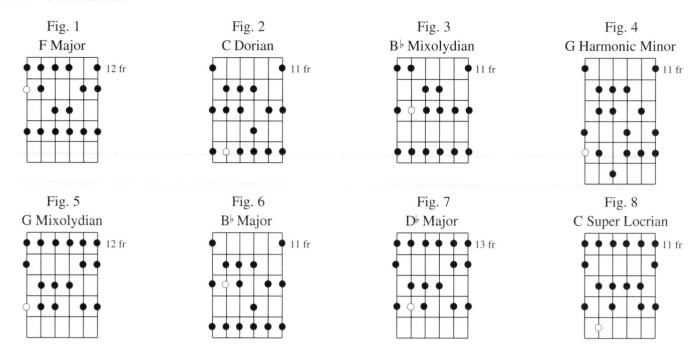

Fig. 1 — F Major — 12 fr
Fig. 2 — C Dorian — 11 fr
Fig. 3 — B♭ Mixolydian — 11 fr
Fig. 4 — G Harmonic Minor — 11 fr

Fig. 5 — G Mixolydian — 12 fr
Fig. 6 — B♭ Major — 11 fr
Fig. 7 — D♭ Major — 13 fr
Fig. 8 — C Super Locrian — 11 fr

Sample Licks for "Confiscation"

Fig. 9

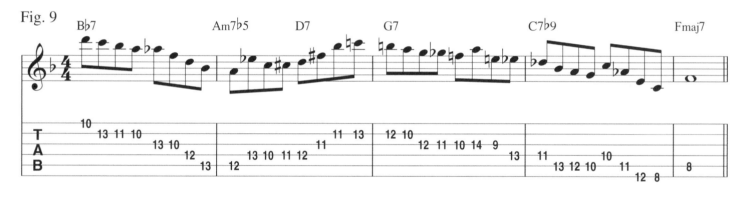

Fig. 10

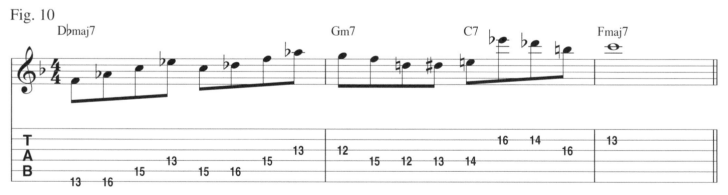

Fig. 11

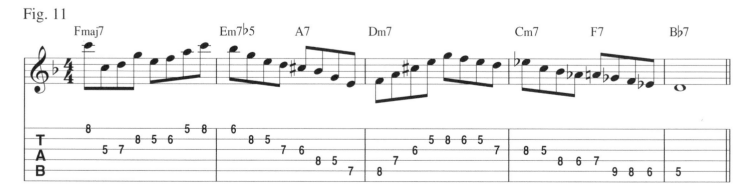

STELLAR

"Stellar" is a 32-bar chart that modulates several times before eventually resolving in B♭ major. One interesting feature of this tune is the large number of "minor ii-V" progressions. The difference between a major ii-V and a minor ii-V is the "ii" chord. In a major ii-V, the ii chord has a minor 7 quality, and in a minor ii-V, the ii chord has a minor 7♭5 quality. Here are the key centers and suggested scales:

Meas. 1-2 (D minor) use Fig. 1, *D harmonic minor*

Meas. 3-4 (B♭ major) use Fig. 2, *C Dorian*

Meas. 5-7 (E♭ major) use Fig. 3, *E♭ major*

Meas. 8 (D♭ major) use Fig. 4, *A♭ Mixolydian*

Meas. 9 (B♭ major) use Fig. 2, *C Dorian*

Meas. 10-11 (D minor) use Fig. 1, *D harmonic minor*

Meas. 12 (A♭ major) use Fig. 5, *A♭ major*

Meas. 13-14 (F major) use Fig. 6, *F major*

Meas. 15-16 (B♭ major) use Fig. 2, *C Dorian*

Meas. 17-18 (C minor) use Fig. 7, *G Super Locrian*

Meas. 19-20 (B♭ major) use Fig. 2, *C Dorian*

Meas. 21-22 (D♭ major) use Fig. 4, *A♭ Mixolydian*

Meas. 23-24 (B♭ major) use Fig. 2, *C Dorian*

Meas. 25-26 (D minor) use Fig. 1, *D harmonic minor*

Meas. 27-28 (C minor) use Fig. 3, *E♭ major*

Meas. 29-30 (B♭ minor) use Fig. 4, *A♭ Mixolydian*

Meas. 31-32 (B♭ major) use Fig. 2, *C Dorian*

Meas. 33-34 (B♭ minor) use Fig. 4, *A♭ Mixolydian*

Meas. 35-36 (B♭ major) use Fig. 2, *C Dorian*

Meas. 37-38 (B♭ minor) use Fig. 4, *A♭ Mixolydian*

Meas. 39-40 (B♭ major) use Fig. 2, *C Dorian*

Meas. 41-42 (B♭ minor) use Fig. 4, *A♭ Mixolydian*

Meas. 43 (F major) use Fig. 6, *F major*

All the sample phrases for this piece exhibit a "roller coaster-like" contour filled with peaks and valleys. This isn't the only way to construct a line, but it is a proven way to build natural and flowing melodic motion into your solos. The first lick (Fig. 8) works against the first four measures of the tune. The second lick (Fig. 9) should be played against measures 13-16, and the final phrase works over measures 25-28.107

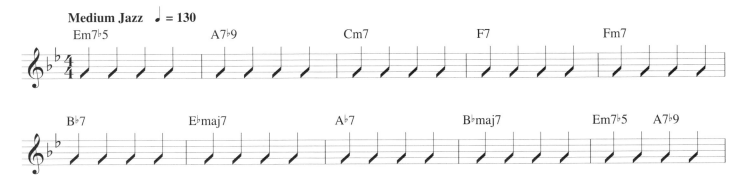

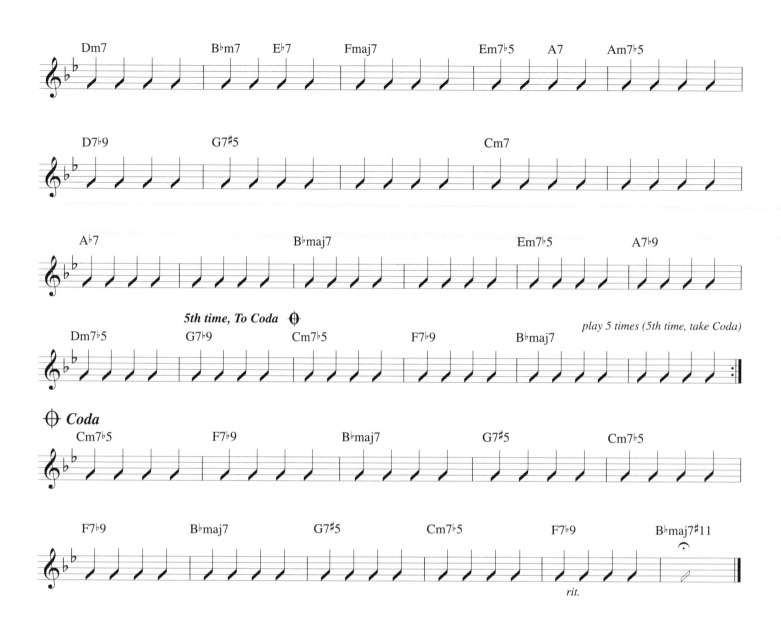

Scales for "Stellar"

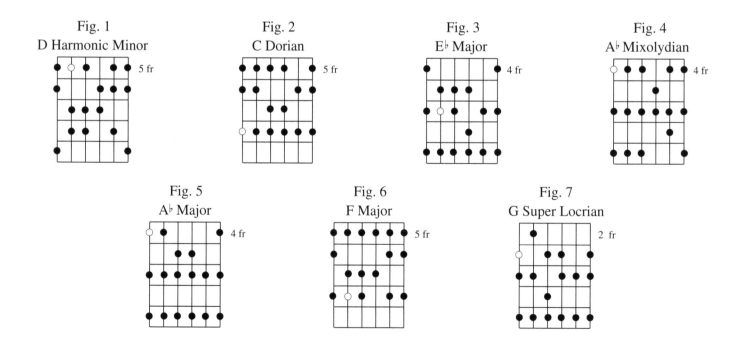

Fig. 1
D Harmonic Minor

Fig. 2
C Dorian

Fig. 3
E♭ Major

Fig. 4
A♭ Mixolydian

Fig. 5
A♭ Major

Fig. 6
F Major

Fig. 7
G Super Locrian

Sample Licks for "Stellar"

Fig. 8

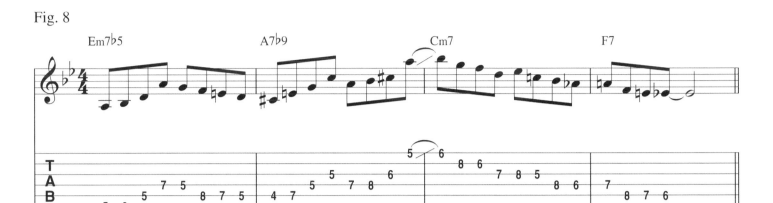

Fig. 9

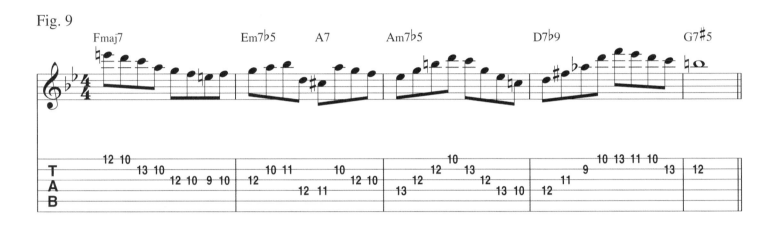

Fig. 10

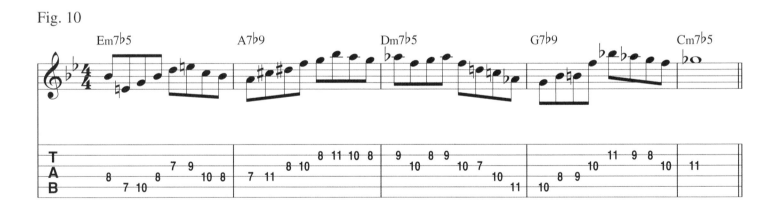

RECORD ME

"Record Me" is a 16-bar tune in A minor with a "Latin" feel. Generally speaking, a "Latin" feel means that the rhythms are influenced by hispanic music. It also means that the eighth and sixteenth notes are played straight and even rather than swung. The modulations and scale choices (not including the intro) are as follows:

Meas. 1-4 (A minor) use Fig. 1, *A melodic minor*

Meas. 5-9 (Bb major) use Fig. 2, *C Dorian*

Meas. 10-11 (Ab major) use Fig. 3, *Ab major*

Meas. 12-13 (Gb major) use Fig. 4, *Gb major*

Meas. 14 (F major) use Fig. 5, *F major*

Meas. 15, beats 1-3 (F major) use Fig. 5, *F major*

Meas. 15, beat 4 (A minor) use Fig. 6, *E Super Locrian*

Meas. 16 (A minor) use Fig. 6, *E Super Locrian*

"Record Me" is a combination of simple one chord vamps, as in measures 1-4, and more complex chord sequences such as bars 9-16. Each of the sample phrases address key changes in the progression. Fig. 7 works over bars 4-5 and utilizes string skip fingerings, Fig. 8 over bars 9-11, and Fig. 9 over measures 15-1.

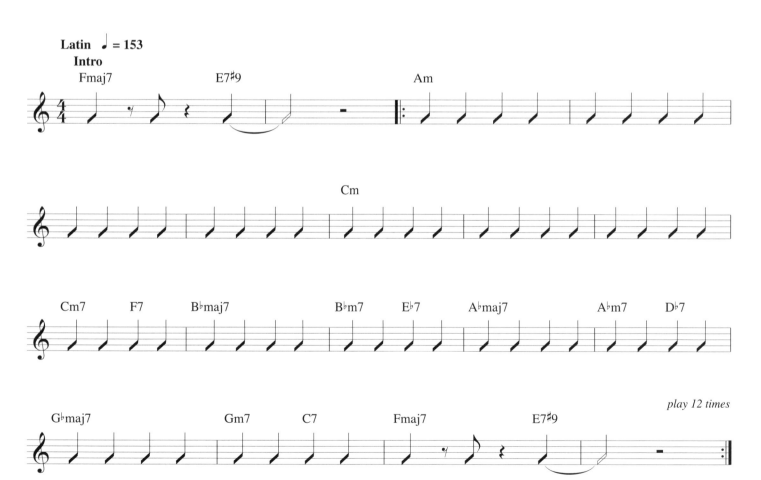

Scales for "Record Me"

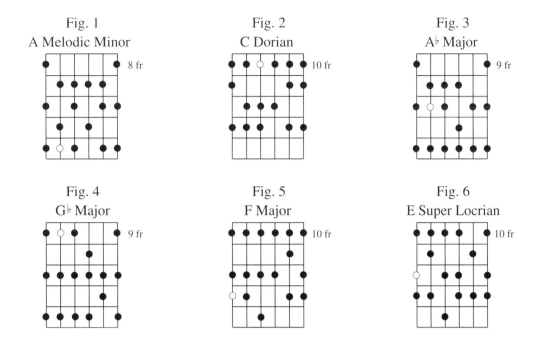

Sample Licks for "Record Me"

Fig. 7

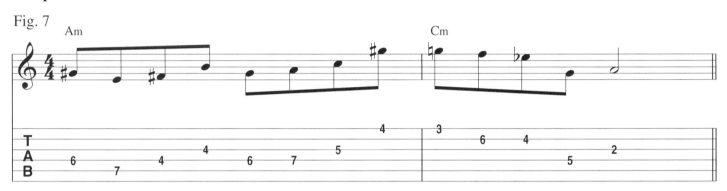

Fig. 8

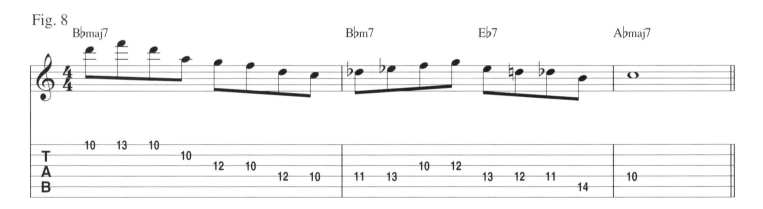

Fig. 9

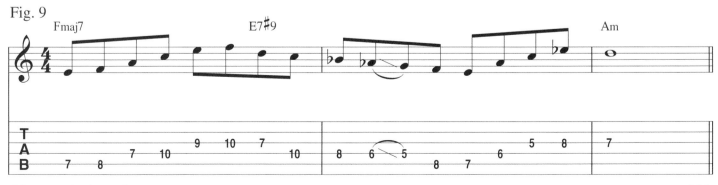

I'VE GOT CHANGES

"I've Got Changes" is based on a common jazz chord progression called "rhythm changes," which in turn gets its name from the popular Gershwin standard, "I've Got Rhythm." Many bebop tunes have been written around this chord progression, which is usually in the key of B♭ major and played at a fairly fast tempo. Here is the harmonic outline for this tune:

A Section
Meas. 1-4 (B♭ major) use Fig. 1, *B♭ major*

Meas. 5 (E♭ major) use Fig. 3, *E♭ major*

Meas. 6, beats 1 and 2 (A♭ major) use Fig. 4, *E♭ Mixolydian*

Meas. 6, beats 3 and 4 use Fig. 5, *E diminished 7th arpeggio*

1st/2nd Ending
Meas. 7-10 (B♭ major) use Fig. 1, *B♭ major*

B Section
Meas. 11-12 (G major) use Fig. 6, *D Mixolydian*

Meas. 13-14 (C major) use Fig. 7, *G Mixolydian*

Meas. 15-16 (F major) use Fig. 8, *C Mixolydian*

A Section
Meas. 17-22 (B♭ major) use Fig. 1, *B♭ major*

Meas. 23 (E♭ major) use Fig. 3, *E♭ major*

Meas. 24, beats 1 and 2 (A♭ major) use Fig. 4, *E♭ Mixolydian*

Meas. 24, beats 3 and 4 use Fig. 5, *E diminished 7th arpeggio*

Meas. 25-26 (B♭ major) use Fig. 1, *B♭ major*

Meas. 27-31 (E♭ major) use Fig. 3, *E♭ major*

The F Super Locrian scale in Fig. 2 can be used as an alternative over all the F7 chords in the piece. The *Super Locrian* scale is sometimes called the *Altered Dominant* scale because it fits so well over altered dominant chords. If you analyze it next to its parallel major scale (in this case the F major scale) it contains the root F, major third A, flat five C♭, sharp five C♯, flat seven E♭, flat nine G♭ and sharp nine G♯.

Fig. 9 is a good example of how to employ arpeggios over the first four measures of the progression. Fig. 10 works over the beginning of the bridge at measures 11-15, and the last phrase (Fig. 11) should be played against bars 5-7. Make sure you observe the articulation markings for these licks. They'll help you handle the fast tempo more easily.

Scales for "I've Got Changes"

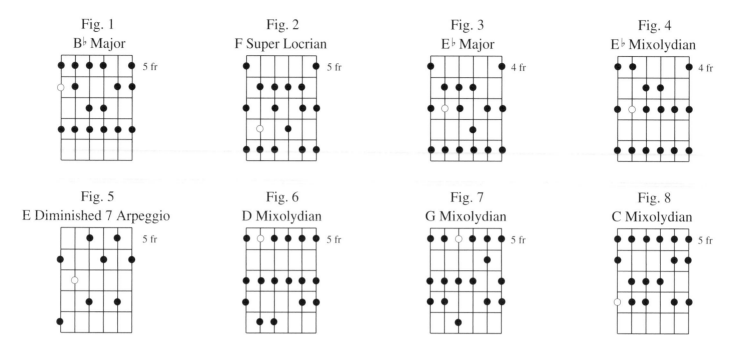

Sample Licks for "I've Got Changes"

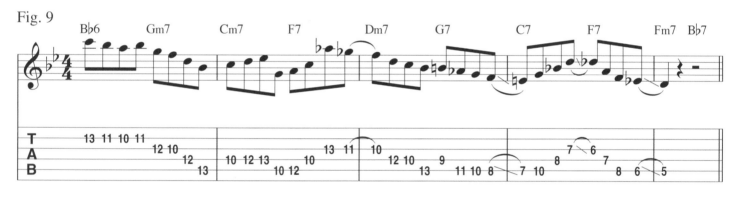

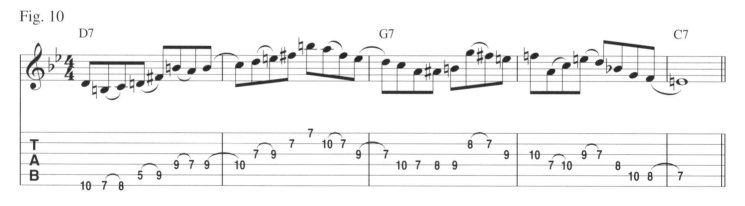

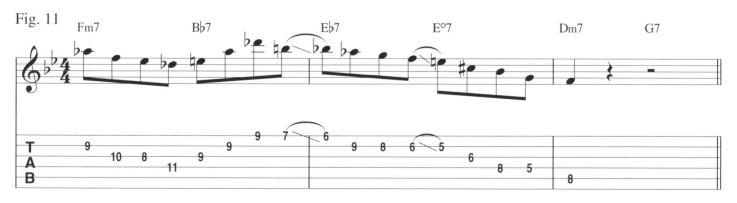

CHAPTER 5: METAL JAMS
INTRODUCTION TO METAL GUITAR

Learning how to improvise is about learning how to create. To be good at it you must know what scales go with what chords, how to break down and interpret different rhythmic feels, and have a well developed vocabulary of stylistic phrases and licks. These are the ingredients that make a great improviser, but how does someone attain these skills?

The best way to develop improvisational skills is to get together and jam with great musicians. However, if you live in a remote area or simply don't know any other musicians to play with, this isn't always possible. That's where these metal jam charts come in. Now you can sit down and jam with great musicians anytime, anywhere and in any style.

All ten tunes have been specially designed to cover a wide variety of the most popular tempos, feels, keys and styles used by the icons of Heavy Metal. Each exercise comes with not only a complete chord chart to guide you along, but also a full analysis of the form, key centers, rhythms, style and specific advice for improvising. Also included are many suggested scales for you to use, as well as three great sample licks of varying levels for you to learn from and incorporate into your own soloing vocabulary. Whether you're a pro or a beginner, the jam charts will take your playing to a higher level with killer-sounding tracks and valuable playing tips.

RACEWAY PARK

"Raceway Park," is a fast, driving track made up of three sections: verse, pre-chorus, and chorus. The verse and chorus are centered around the A blues scale while the pre-chorus is centered around the E blues scale. This recurring key change (A to E) presents a constant challenge to begin a phrase in one key and end it in another. For this reason, I have placed all scale diagrams in the same position. This will allow you to change keys more gracefully and with less thought. Along with the A and E blues scales (Figs. 1 and 4), I have also included the A Dorian scale (Fig. 2) and the B♭ major scale (Fig. 3). The A Dorian scale should be used along with the A blues scale during the verse and chorus sections. The B♭ major scale is an optional scale that you can use over the held E♭5 chord in the verse.

It's important to understand that the scales I have provided you with are not the only ones that will work. They are, in my opinion, the most obvious and commonly used given this particular style and chord progression, however your ear should always be the final judge. If you want to experiment, try adding a few chromatic notes, (notes that are not in the scale) to the scale fingerings in Figs. 1-4. As long as you don't hold these notes, they will usually work quite well.

Rhythmically, the verse and chorus have a "straight-eighth" feel (because the primary rhythms are built around eighth notes) while the pre-chorus is more syncopated and funky. My advice is to think in eighth notes at first, and then try incorporating a few faster triplet phrases when you feel up to it. For this track I have also included three sample phrases utilizing the A blues scale: one easy (Fig. 5), one medium (Fig. 6) and one hard (Fig. 7). Play each lick a few times, then try using them in context with your own ideas. Learning how to personalize musical phrases is crucial to assimilating them into your soloing vocabulary.

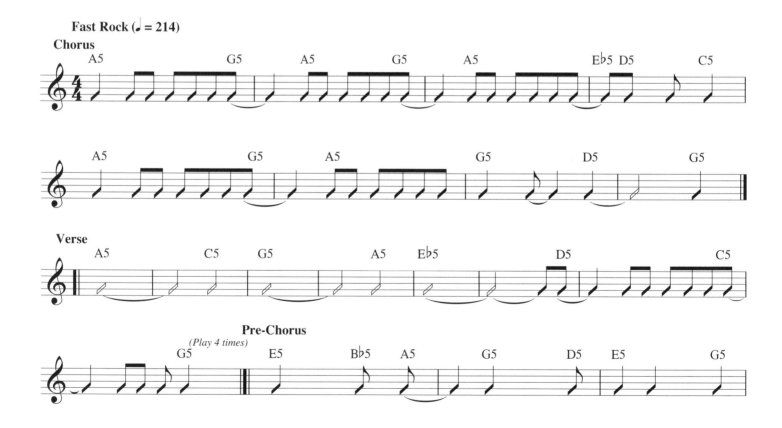

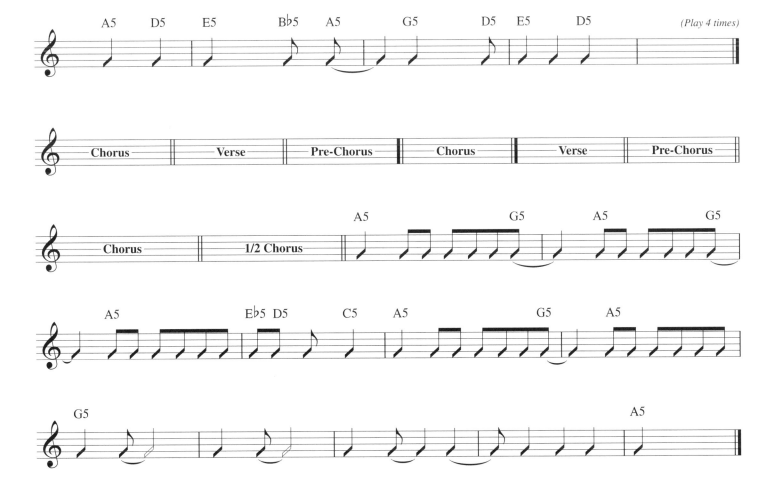

Scales for "Raceway Park"

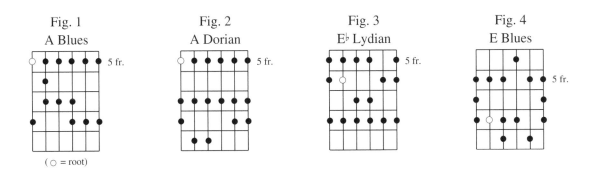

Fig. 1
A Blues

Fig. 2
A Dorian

Fig. 3
E♭ Lydian

Fig. 4
E Blues

(○ = root)

Sample Licks for "Raceway Park"

Fig. 5 A Blues

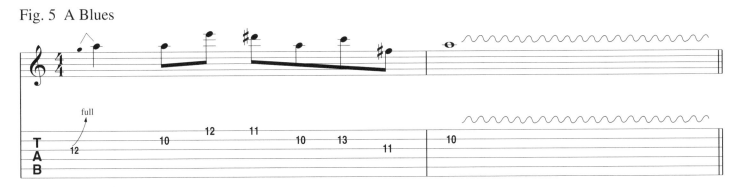

Fig. 6 A Blues

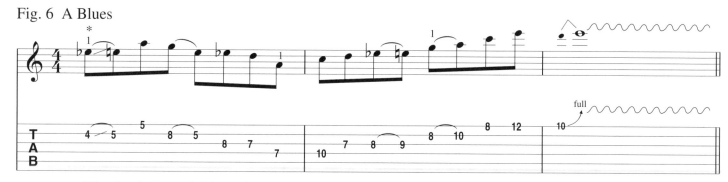

*Number indicates left hand fingerings throughout the book.

Fig. 7 A Blues

SHOCK TREATMENT

This track is built around four sections: verse, pre-chorus, chorus and an additional bridge played only once at the end. The verse, chorus and bridge are centered around the E blues scale while the pre-chorus is centered around F♯ blues. You can use the E blues and E Aeolian scales (Figs. 1 and 2) for the verse, chorus and bridge and the F♯ blues and F♯ Dorian scale (Figs. 4 and 5) for the pre-chorus. The E Locrian scale (Fig. 3) sounds good against the B♭5 chord in the verse but it's not essential that you use it.

As you read through each track you may notice that there are occasionally chords which don't seem to make sense against the scales I've given you. An example of this would be the F5 chord which appears in the fourth beat of the second measure of the pre-chorus. Even though you are improvising in F♯ this chord will not create a problem for you, because it only sounds momentarily between two chords (E5 and F♯5) which do work with the scale. Chords like these are referred to as passing chords.

I would describe the feel of this track as "pounding" and "quarter note heavy". There is also an underlying sixteenth-note pulse behind the quarter note feel which adds a slight "funkiness" to the track. Although the tempo is not fast, you may find it difficult to groove hard on your faster phrases. I recommend practicing your scales in sixteenth notes and then trying them in sixteenth note triplets. You can also try ignoring the feel of the track altogether and play "out of time" which will give you tremendous rhythmic freedom.

I've included three sample phrases for you to try against the track. The first two (Figs. 6 and 7) will work during the verse, chorus, and bridge, and the third (Fig. 8) works in the pre-chorus. Although the sample licks are written to fit over specific sections, you can use them anywhere by simply transposing them to a different key. For example; by playing Figs. 6 and 7 up two frets from where they're written, you can use them during the pre-chorus. Likewise, by playing Fig. 8 two frets lower than written, you can use it over the verse, chorus, and bridge.

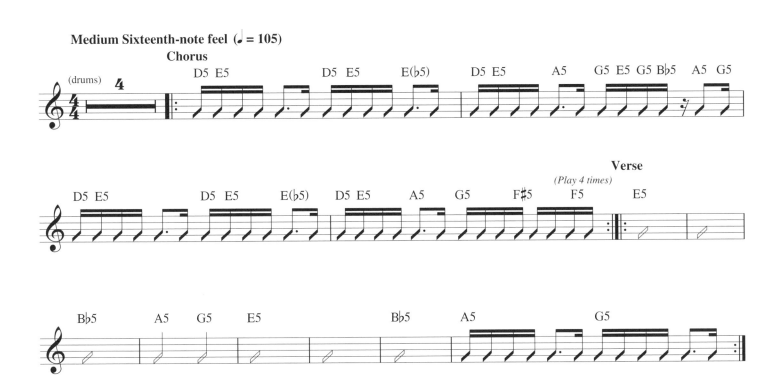

Pre-Chorus

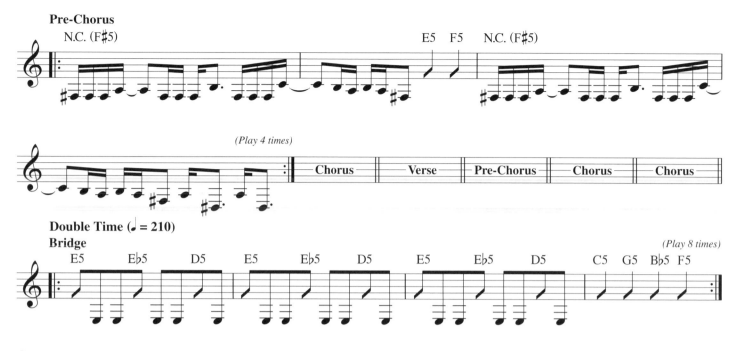

(Play 4 times)

| Chorus | Verse | Pre-Chorus | Chorus | Chorus |

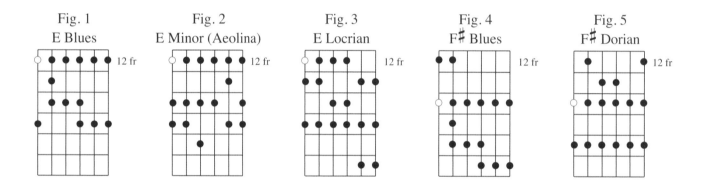

Double Time (♩ = 210)
Bridge

(Play 8 times)

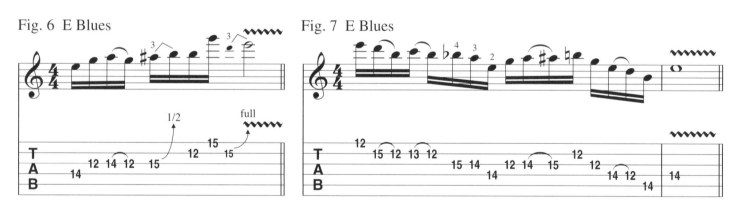

Scales for "Shock Treatment"

Fig. 1	Fig. 2	Fig. 3	Fig. 4	Fig. 5
E Blues	E Minor (Aeolina)	E Locrian	F♯ Blues	F♯ Dorian

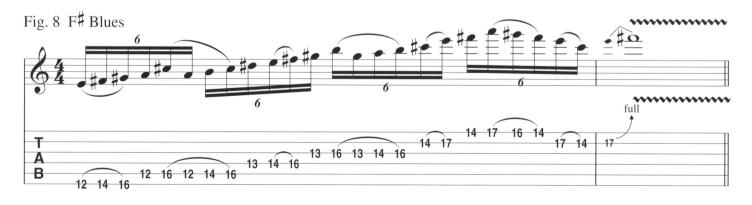

Sample Licks for "Shock Treatment"

Fig. 6 E Blues

Fig. 7 E Blues

Fig. 8 F♯ Blues

SADDLE UP

The aptly titled "Saddle Up" is constructed with a verse, pre-chorus and chorus. The verse and chorus have a D Phrygian/D blues quality, however the pre-chorus is derived from the interesting E Spanish Phrygian scale. The Spanish Phrygian scale is the fifth mode of the harmonic minor scale, in this case A harmonic minor. If you were to compare a Spanish Phrygian scale to a regular Phrygian scale you would see that all the notes were the same except for the third note which is one-half step higher in Spanish Phrygian than in regular phrygian. Spanish Phrygian also tends to have a "classical" quality because of it's relationship to harmonic minor.

For this chart you are given four scales: two fingerings for the D blues scale, one D Phrygian scale and one E Spanish Phrygian. The D blues and D Phrygian scales work great over the verse and chorus and the E Spanish Phrygian covers the pre-chorus. You should also be aware that during the last measure of the pre-chorus, over the G5, A5 and C5 chords, you can go back to using the D blues scale. This will melodically anticipate (or foreshadow) the following chorus.

The title for this tune comes from the "gallop-like" feel of the chorus. The pre-chorus however, is in what's known as a half-time feel. This term is used because the beats feel as if they are happening at half the speed of the previous section. The moderate tempo of this track should allow your lines to come out smoothly and easily. As an exercise, try playing each of the scales in eighth notes, then triplets and finally sixteenth notes. This will help you to be more creative with your rhythmic phrasing.

Again, three sample licks are provided. The first and third (Figs. 5 and 7) are for the chorus and verse, and the second (Fig. 6) is for the pre-chorus. To play it smoothly, make sure you anticipate the position changes in Fig. 7.

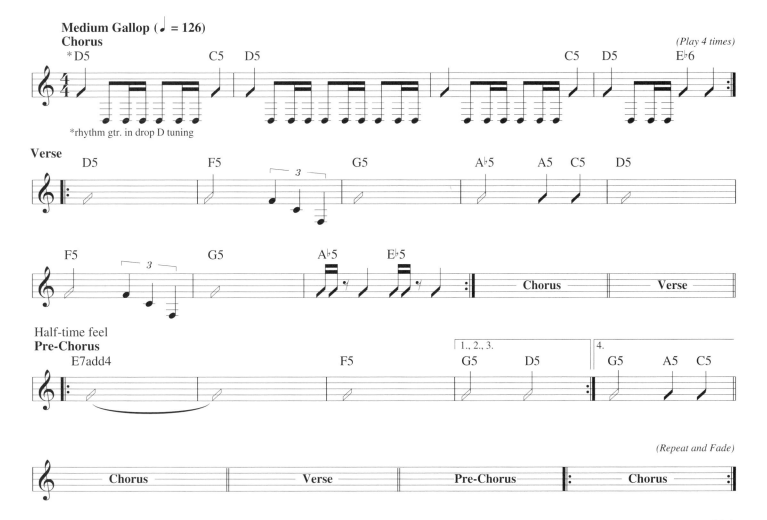

Scales for "Saddle Up"

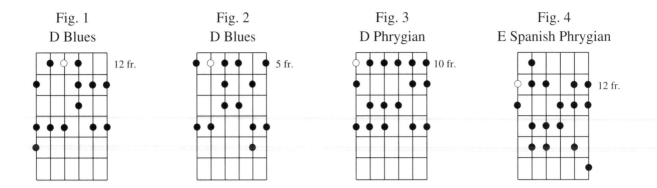

Fig. 1
D Blues

Fig. 2
D Blues

Fig. 3
D Phrygian

Fig. 4
E Spanish Phrygian

Sample Licks for "Saddle Up"

Fig. 5 D Blues

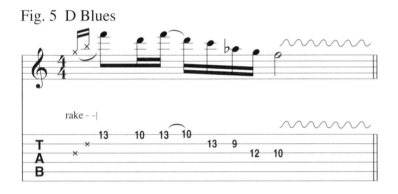

Fig. 6 E Spanish Phrygian

Fig. 7 D Blues

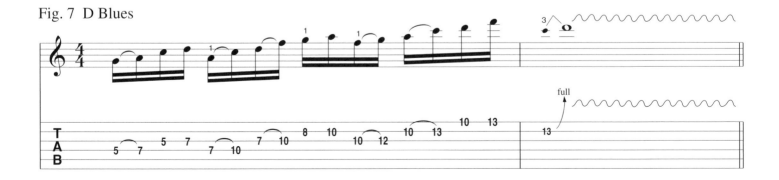

Forward March

"Forward March" is comprised of three parts. Each part is based primarily on the C blues/C Dorian sound. The one possible exception to this is the first chord of the bridge, G5. You can use the C blues scale over this chord or you can treat it seperately and try the G dominant pentatonic scale in Fig. 5. This scale is similar to the G minor pentatonic except that the second note is one- half step higher in the dominant version. Another option is to use the G major pentatonic scale in Fig. 3. Either way, you must make sure to return to the C blues or C Dorian scales by the next measure. For this tune there are two fingerings for the C blues scale: a low one (Fig. 1) and a high one (Fig. 4). This will give your improvisations a wider range and greater dynamics.

The slow, dirge-like tempo of this cut creates a big, open, spacious feeling and should afford you plenty of rhythmic leeway for improvising. In general, slower tempos tend to present more rhythmic options whereas faster tempos are usually more constraining. The important thing when soloing is to change the pace of your phrases now and then to hold the listener's attention.

In the first lick (Fig. 6) you must bend two notes up in different amounts simultaneously. The best way to do this is to place your third finger on the 10th fret of the G string with your second and first fingers on the 9th and 8th frets respectively, and your fourth finger on the 10th fret of the B string by itself. This will naturally cause you to bend the G string farther than the B string. In the third lick (Fig. 8) there are a series of four sextuplets. The first two are primarily blues based but the third and fourth incorporate triads taken from the C Dorian scale. In order, these triads are: C minor, B♭ major and G minor.

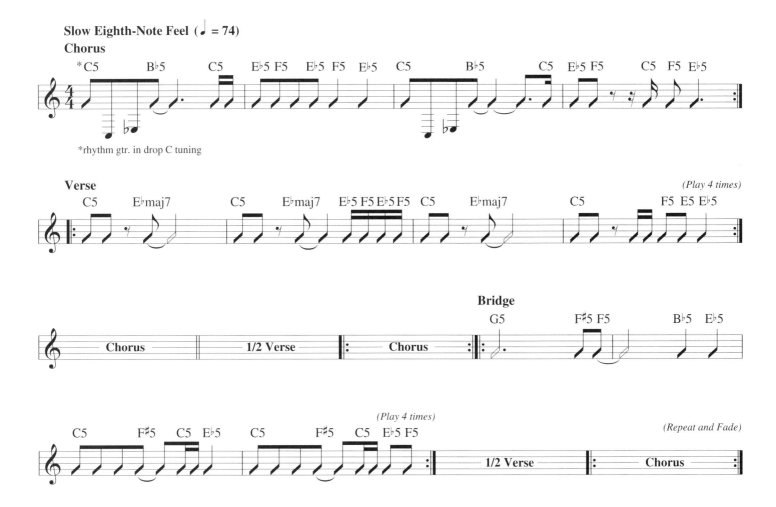

Scales for "Forward March"

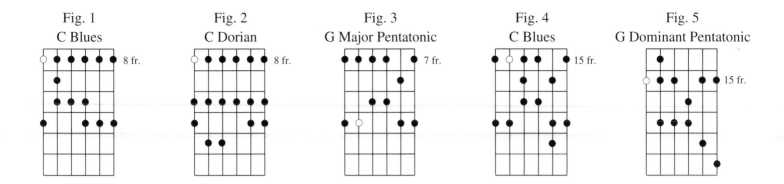

Fig. 1
C Blues

Fig. 2
C Dorian

Fig. 3
G Major Pentatonic

Fig. 4
C Blues

Fig. 5
G Dominant Pentatonic

Sample Licks for "Forward March"

Fig. 6 C Blues

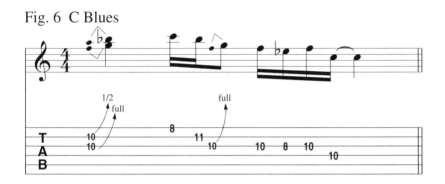

Fig. 7 C Blues

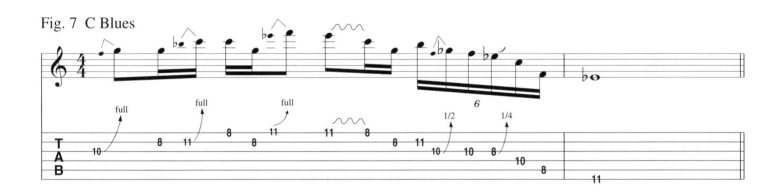

Fig. 8 C Blues / Dorian

POLKA TIME

This chart is broken down into four sections, all of which are centered around the F♯ Aeolian or "natural minor" scale. F♯ Aeolian is the sixth mode of the A major scale, which means it has the same notes as A major but its primary note or root has been shifted to F♯. You can also use the F♯ minor pentatonic scale because the notes of this scale are contained within the notes of F♯ Aeolian. As in the previous tune, the scales provided are written in two different places on the fingerboard to allow greater mobility.

The main challange with this exercise is its unrelentingly fast tempo. To play comfortably at tempos like this requires good technical facility and unwavering concentration. You should also try to pace yourself, perhaps starting off very simply with a few held notes, slowly working your way into the groove. Another hint is to tap your foot on the half note or every two beats instead of on the quarter note. This will help make the groove seem less uptight and more flowing. Also, don't feel "bound" by the tempo. Try playing in and around it, or disregard it completely and just play where you feel most comfortable. If you really feel at a loss for ideas, listen to what others have done with grooves like this. Bands like Metallica, Pantera, Anthrax and others have written many tunes at this tempo. You will probably never be asked to improvise on a tune like this for a full five minutes straight with no break. But just in case, you'll be ready.

Last, but not least, make sure to check out the sample licks and good luck!

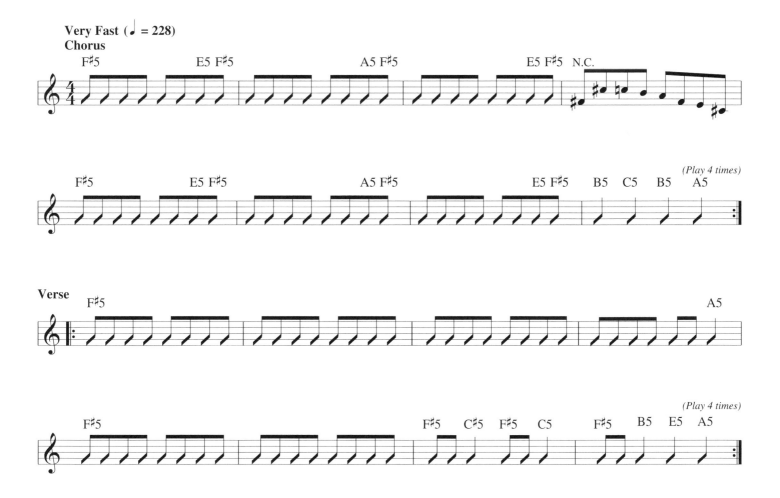

Pre-Chorus

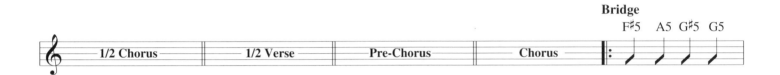

Scales for "Polka Time"

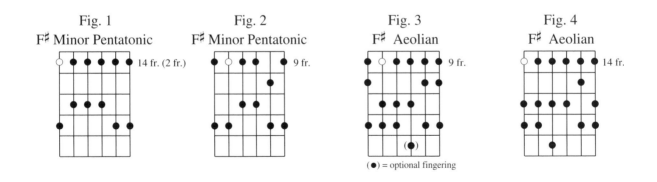

Fig. 1 F# Minor Pentatonic — 14 fr. (2 fr.)

Fig. 2 F# Minor Pentatonic — 9 fr.

Fig. 3 F# Aeolian — 9 fr.

Fig. 4 F# Aeolian — 14 fr.

(●) = optional fingering

Sample Licks for "Polka Time"

Fig. 5 F♯ Minor Pentatonic

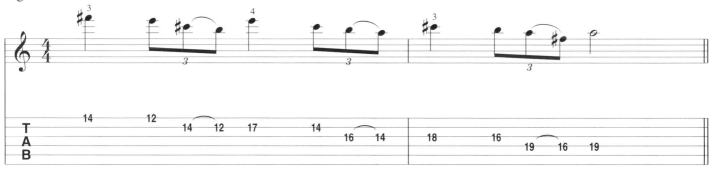

Fig. 6 F♯ Minor Pentatonic

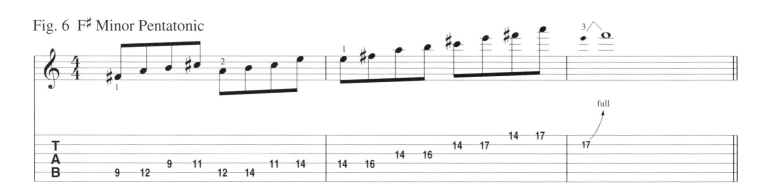

Fig. 7 F♯ Aeolian

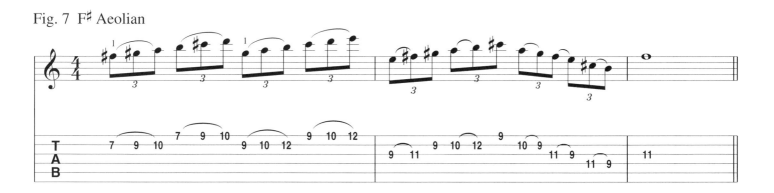

SHAKIN' THE BOOT

From the beginning to the end the dominating tonality here is B Dorian. Since this is the case, you may also use the B minor pentatonic or B blues scale. It's also important to notice that the Bm13 chord in the chorus contains the defining or critical notes of B Dorian: D and G♯. In other words, there is no other Dorian scale that contains those two notes. The scales I have chosen to include for this track are two fingerings of B minor pentatonic, one B Dorian and one B blues. The second version of B minor pentatonic (Fig. 2) is an extended fingering which is very useful for moving up and down the fingerboard. Try practicing it with sliding and without.

Rhythmically, this track is the funkiest of the bunch. Its strong sixteenth-note feel is characteristic of songs by bands like The Red Hot Chili Peppers, Living Colour, and Fishbone. Its medium tempo allows the groove to feel relaxed and open sounding while still retaining a degree of heaviness. It's important that you learn to lock into the sixteenth-note feel with your phrasing. You might want to start off by playing the scales up and down in eighth notes (two notes per beat), and then progress to sixteenths (four notes per beat). I also recommend tapping your foot while you are improvising, but this is optional.

Let's take a look at the sample licks. The first one (Fig. 5) is fairly straight forward except for the slight stretch on the pull-offs. The second lick (Fig. 6) requires you to shift positions through the extended pentatonic scale in Fig. 2. Make sure you anticipate the jump with your first finger. The last lick (Fig. 7) involves string skipping and wide intervals through the B dorian scale. Although I've included specific articulation markings (hammer-ons, pull-offs, etc.) for each lick in this book, feel free to play them any way you want.

Scales for "Shakin' the Boot"

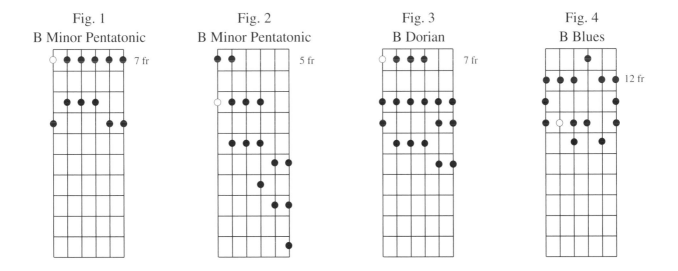

Fig. 1
B Minor Pentatonic

Fig. 2
B Minor Pentatonic

Fig. 3
B Dorian

Fig. 4
B Blues

Sample Licks for "Shakin' the Boot"

Fig. 5 B Dorian

Fig. 6 B Minor Pentatonic

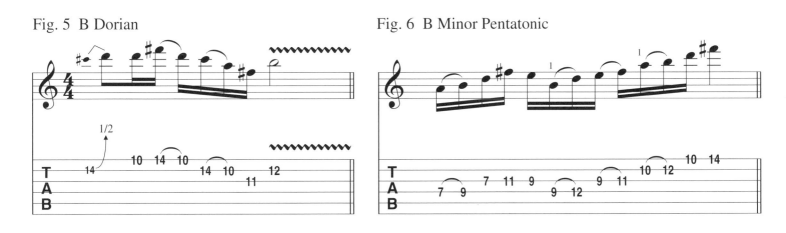

Fig. 7 B Dorian

SHUFFLIN'

"Shufflin'" has four sections: verse, chorus, bridge and interlude. The verse, chorus and interlude are very similar and all resolve to either D blues (Fig. 1) or D Phrygian (Fig. 2). The bridge however, is based more around A Phrygian (Fig. 3), although the D blues scale will work here as well. As with many rock and metal songs, there is often uncertainty as to which scale is the true backbone of the progression. In most cases you can use several different scales without any problem. A good example of this is the E♭5 chord in the fourth measure of the bridge. Here you could use the D blues or D Phrygian scale, or you could try the A super Locrian (Fig. 4) or E♭ major pentatonic scale (Fig. 5). The bottom line is to use your ear and good judgement to determine for yourself which one sounds the best.

Like the title says, this track is a shuffle. The splitting of each main beat into three even "sub-beats" is what makes a shuffle feel the way it does. Most shuffles are written with a 12/8 time signature; the main pulse occurring on beats 1, 4, 7, and 10 with the sub-pulses falling in between. If you're not sure what a time signature is, think of a shuffle as four beats in a measure with each beat split into triplets. While shuffles are more common in blues and jazz, they do make there way into rock and metal. The Metallica song "Don't Tread on Me" is an example of a shuffle in a heavy metal context. If you don't read music, put the track on and as you listen, try to follow the music in this booklet with your eyes. You can learn what the notes and symbols mean by making the connection between what you see in the book and what you hear in the track.

The licks in Figs. 6 and 7 work well over the verse and chorus, while Fig. 8 is designed for the bridge. Fig. 8 may be difficult for you at this tempo, so practice it slowly and work your way up.

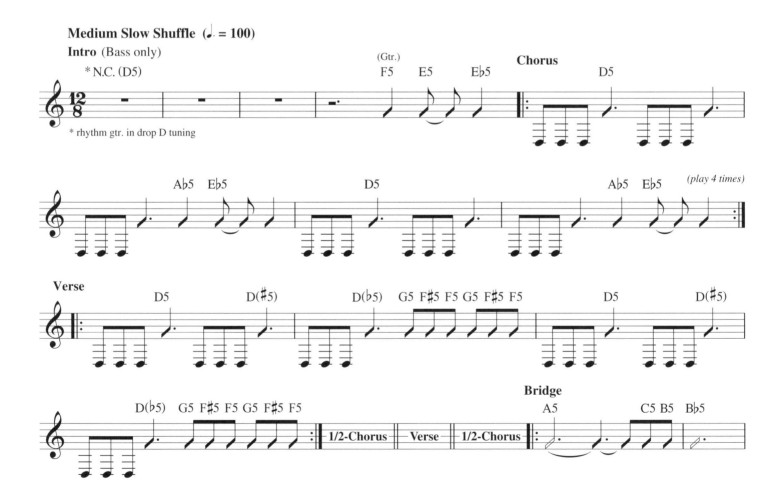

Scales for "Shufflin'"

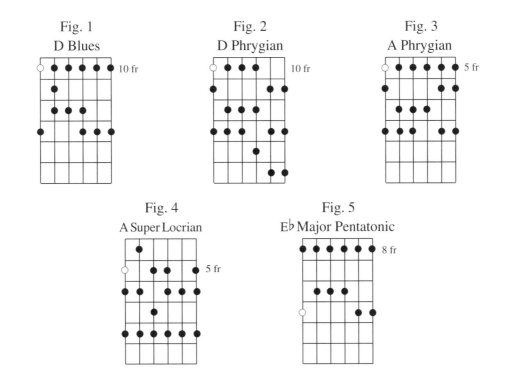

Fig. 1
D Blues
10 fr

Fig. 2
D Phrygian
10 fr

Fig. 3
A Phrygian
5 fr

Fig. 4
A Super Locrian
5 fr

Fig. 5
E♭ Major Pentatonic
8 fr

Sample licks for "Shufflin'"

Fig. 6   D Blues

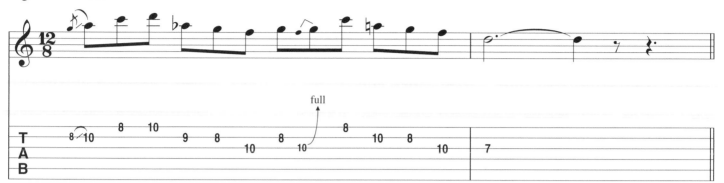

Fig. 7   D Phrygian

Fig. 8   A Phrygian

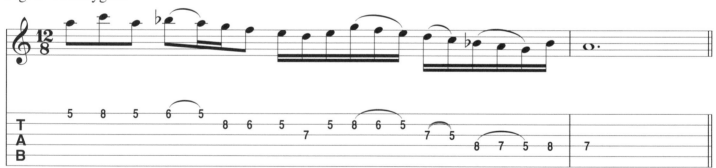

HELLBOYS FROM COW

Practicing with this chart will challange your ability to change scales in midstream. Though the form is straight forward, there are a number of key changes to watch out for. The E blues scale is the main scale of choice for the chorus. Over the verse you could continue with E blues or use E Phrygian which sounds particularly well against the F5 chord. The first real change happens at the pre-chorus. Here you should switch to A minor pentatonic for the first four measures and then D minor pentatonic over the last four. One goal you should have as an improviser is to be able to switch scales in the middle of a phrase. In this case, that means starting an idea in A minor pentatonic and finishing it in D minor pentatonic. The only way to do this smoothly and consistantly is to know the scales inside and out and to anticipate the change before it happens. This may take some time and effort, but it's well worth it! Another change occurs in the bridge which begins with B minor pentatonic for the first two measures, changes to F Lydian for the second two measures and then back to B minor pentatonic for the last four bars.

"Hellboys from Cow" has a 16th-note feel with a strong emphasis on the quarter note. The chorus is slightly funky and syncopated while the other sections have a more straight ahead "metal" feel. The bridge goes into "double time" where the tempo is twice as fast as the other sections. (This is why the lick in Fig. 10 is written in eighth notes.)

The sample lick in Fig. 8 comes from the E minor pentatonic scale fingering in Fig. 1. Fig. 9 is a position changing lick in A minor pentatonic, and Fig. 10 switches from B minor pentatonic to F Lydian and back.

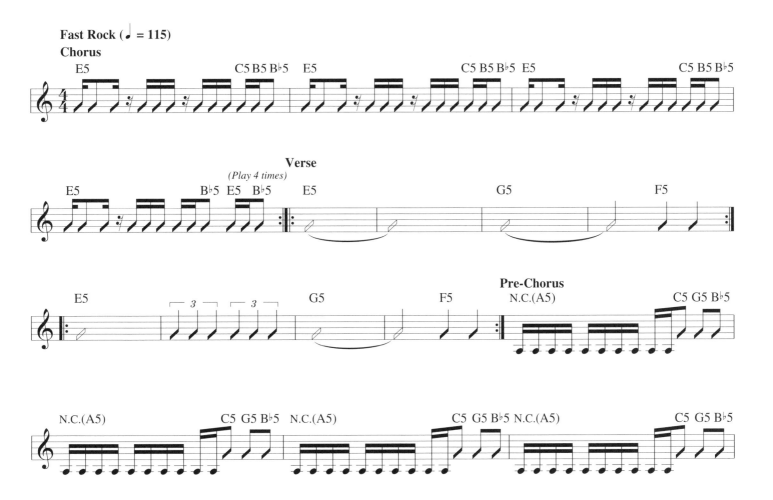

Scales for "Hellboys from Cow"

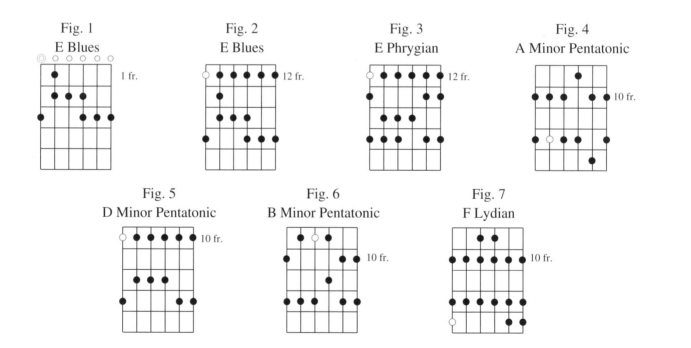

Fig. 1
E Blues

Fig. 2
E Blues

Fig. 3
E Phrygian

Fig. 4
A Minor Pentatonic

Fig. 5
D Minor Pentatonic

Fig. 6
B Minor Pentatonic

Fig. 7
F Lydian

Sample Licks for "Hellboys from Cow"

Fig. 8 E Blues

Fig. 9 A Minor Pentatonic

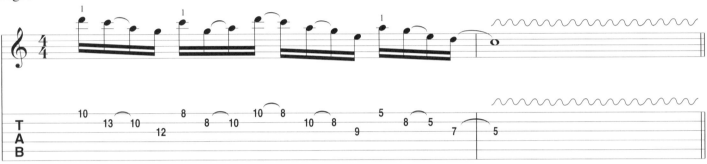

Fig. 10 B Minor Pentatonic ---------------------------------- F Lydian ------------------------------------

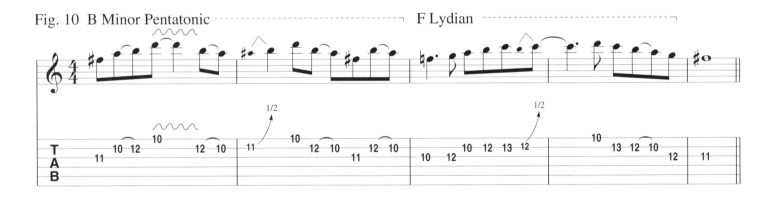

ODDLY ENOUGH

Like the previous tune, this one moves through many different scale changes. The verse and riff 1 both alternate between C♯ blues (Fig. 1) and B♭ blues (Fig. 2). The entire chorus is also centered around C♯ blues but the pre-chorus is where the fun really begins. The pre-chorus is actually a four measure chord, sequence that is repeated three times, each time a whole step higher than before. So for the first chord A5, you can use the A major pentatonic scale (Fig. 3), and for the second chord F5, use F major pentatonic (Fig. 4). Then when you get to the third chord, B5, you should take the fingering in Fig. 3 and play it two frets higher. The same goes for the fourth chord, G5, where you will play Fig. 4 two frets higher. This process is then repeated two more times until the end of the pre-chorus. You may find this challanging and confusing at first, but be patient. If you do this correctly (and your ear will tell you!), your hand should move up one fret for each chord.

The name, "Oddly Enough," comes from the recurring "odd meter" found throughout the tune. An odd meter occurs when the total number of beats in a measure equals an odd number. Five beats per measure and seven beats per measure are the most common odd meters. (Three beats per measure is actually the most common, but because of its frequent use it was given the name "waltz" and is not considered a true odd meter.) During the verse and pre-chorus the measures alternate from 4/4 time to 7/8 time. This means that the 7/8 measures are one eighth note shorter in duration than the 4/4 measures. This periodic switch between even and odd measures creates a rhythmic "hiccup" that may throw you off initially. To help keep your place, try tapping your foot only on the first beat of each measure. Don't try to play while you're doing this, just focus your attention on where beat one is. Another odd meter to watch out for occurs on every fourth measure of the chorus, shifting from 6/8 time to 5/8 time.

The first two sample licks will help you learn to phrase across the meter change. The third lick is a cool position changer that works over the chorus.

Scales for "Oddly Enough"

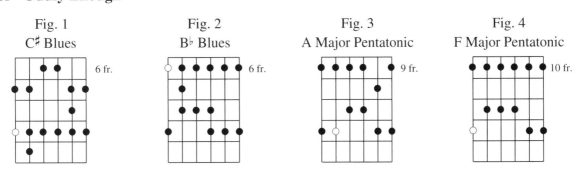

Fig. 1
C♯ Blues

Fig. 2
B♭ Blues

Fig. 3
A Major Pentatonic

Fig. 4
F Major Pentatonic

Sample Licks for "Oddly Enough"

Fig. 5   C♯ Blues

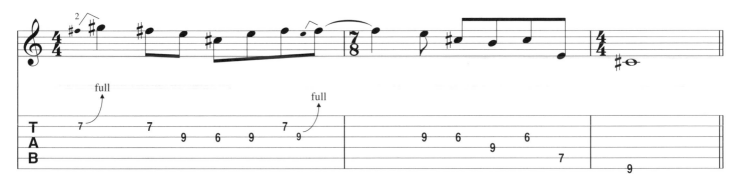

Fig. 6   B♭ Blues

Fig. 7   C♯ Blues

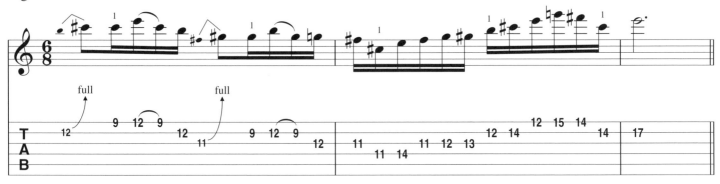

Oddly Enough

Underworld

"Underworld" is made up of four parts. Like previous tracks, each part allows for several scale options. The first and most important scales are F blues and F minor pentatonic, which work over every section of the track. For the pre-chorus you can add B♭ Mixolydian to your choice of scales, however the chorus is where you have the most options. For the first chord of the chorus, G5, you can use either the G blues scale or the D minor pentatonic scale. My suggestion for the second chord, F♯5, is to use the F♯ major pentatonic scale (Figs. 6 and 7). The fingering in Fig. 4 is designed to lead into Fig. 6, just as Fig. 5 leads to Fig. 7. The third and fourth measures of the chorus bring you back to the F blues and F minor pentatonic scales.

The rhythmic feel of this track is a relaxed, medium tempo, straight-eighth rock groove. This type of feel should allow you to really stretch out and go for new ideas regardless of your technical abilities. Remember it's not the number of notes you play, but how cleverly you arrange them that counts. A good improviser never runs out of ideas because he sees each moment as a distinctly different challenge requiring a different approach.

The first two sample phrases for this track work against the entire progression, while the third phrase is designed to be used specifically over the first chord of the chorus (G5) leading into the second (F♯5). Remember that you can always take sample licks from one track and transpose them to work against other tracks. For example if you take Fig. 7 from the second track, "Shock Treatment," and play it one fret higher than written, it'll work over this track. Try this with other licks! Experiment!! Go nuts!!!

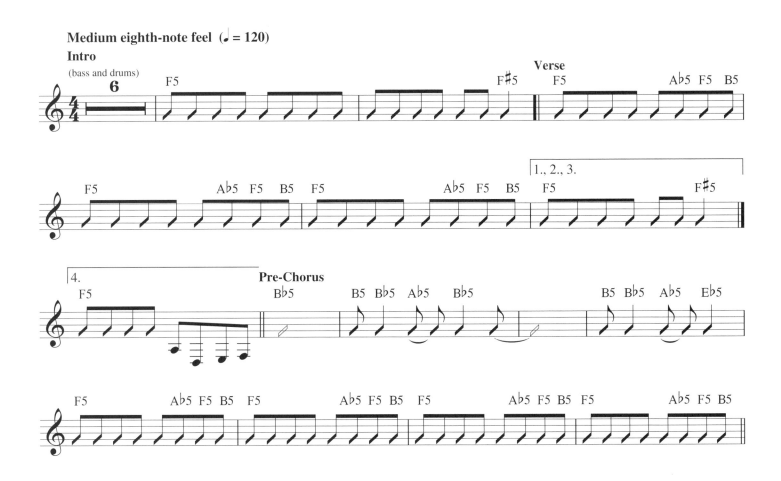

Scales for "Underworld"

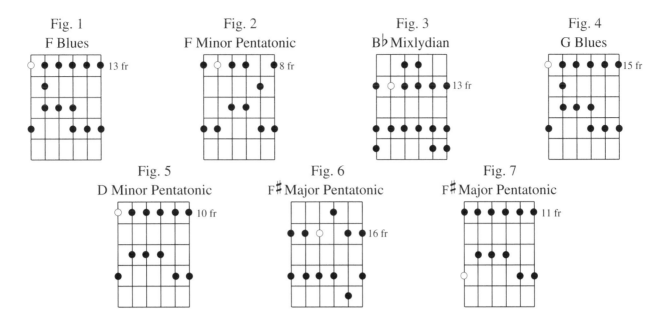

Fig. 1
F Blues

Fig. 2
F Minor Pentatonic

Fig. 3
B♭ Mixlydian

Fig. 4
G Blues

Fig. 5
D Minor Pentatonic

Fig. 6
F♯ Major Pentatonic

Fig. 7
F♯ Major Pentatonic

Sample Licks for "Underworld"

Fig. 7   F Blues

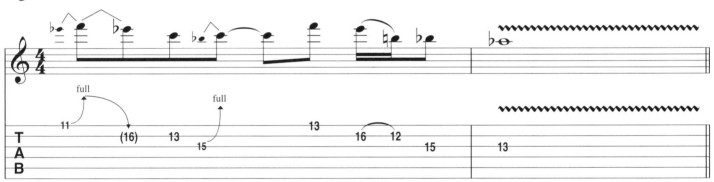

Fig. 8   F Minor Pentatonic

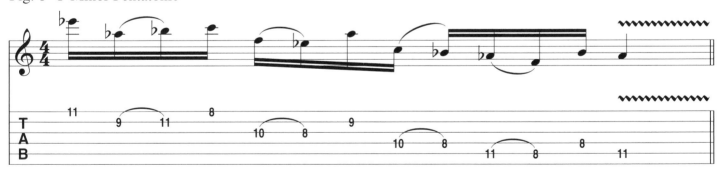

Fig. 9   G Blues

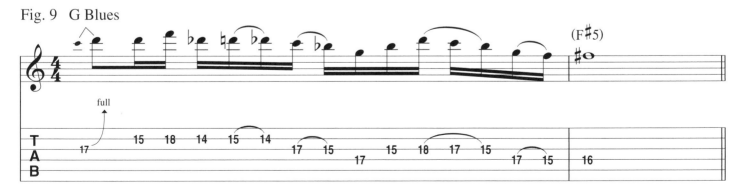

CHAPTER 6: ROCK JAMS
INTRODUCTION TO ROCK GUITAR

In the sixty-plus years it has been around, rock and roll has come to mean different things to different people. So many styles have emerged under the name "rock" that the term itself is practically meaningless. If there is one thing that has defined the sound of rock over the years, it is the electric guitar. From Chuck Berry to George Harrison to Hendrix to Van Halen and beyond, the electric guitar has always been the sonic focal point of this genre.

One of the most important and defining elements in rock is the guitar solo. Just as it is in jazz, blues, and country, the guitar solo is where the guitarist has the opportunity to bring the music to an emotional peak and communicate to the audience in a very immediate and visceral manner. It is also a point in the song where anything can happen, so the guitarist must be able to improvise and react to what is musically happening around him.

To be a good improviser, a guitarist must have the necessary skills and knowledge to express his musical ideas at the moment they come to him. This means he or she should possess a good understanding of the fingerboard (i.e. scales and arpeggios) as well as the technical facility needed to execute his or her ideas (i.e. good picking, hammering-on and pulling-off, and string bending). It is also important to be familiar with what others have done in the genre and to possess a large vocabulary of musical phrases that can be adapted to different situations. And of course it is essential to develop your creative instincts by actually improvising against a variety of musical backdrops.

Each of the ten rock tunes are representative of a different style or groove used in the rock songs of today as well as the past. Along with each chart there is valuable advice and information that will help you to improvise better and with greater confidence. Each exercise also comes with useful scale fingerings and three sample licks that you can learn and incorporate into your own vocabulary of ideas. These licks are clearly written out in standard notation and tablature and are demonstrated for you on the accompanying streaming audio track.

ROLLING CROWS

"Rolling Crows" is comprised of three sections which are all based around the B minor blues scale. You may use any or all of the suggested scale fingerings for the B minor blues scale in Figs. 1, 2, and 3 over the entire track. Fig. 4, *F♯ minor blues*, is a good alternative scale to use over any of the F♯ chords in the tune. Remember that you can move any of these scale fingerings twelve frets above or below where they are written to give you greater range.

The sample phrases in Figs. 5-7 can be played over any part of the chart. In Fig. 5 you must bend E on the ninth fret of the G string up a whole step and keep it bent while playing A on the tenth fret of the B string. The two bends in fig. 6 are both half steps, so make sure you don't bend the strings too far. Fig. 7 utilizes several hammer-ons and pull-offs to create a smooth and flowing articulation. It's a good idea to observe the hammer-on and pull-off markings notated for the various sample licks. Once you've mastered each phrase you may then experiment by trying to pick every note or hammer-on and pull-off to notes that are not marked as such.

Scales for "Rolling Crows"

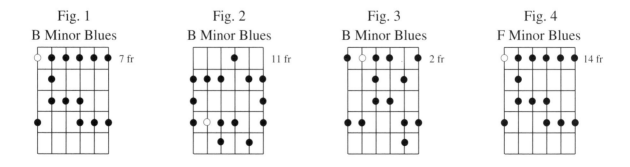

Fig. 1
B Minor Blues
7 fr

Fig. 2
B Minor Blues
11 fr

Fig. 3
B Minor Blues
2 fr

Fig. 4
F Minor Blues
14 fr

Sample Licks for "Rolling Crows"

Fig. 5

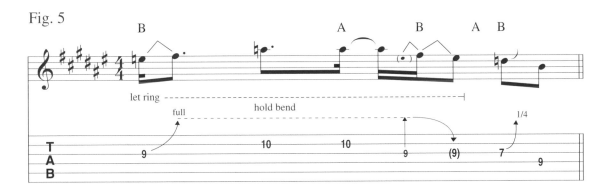

Fig. 6

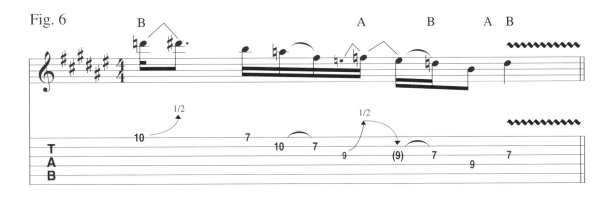

Fig.7

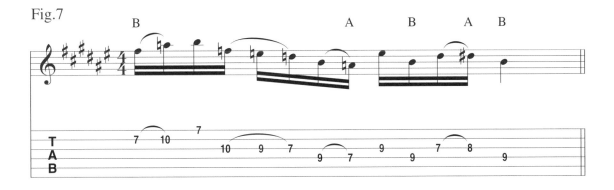

YOUNG AGNES

This tune is influenced by the songs and styles of the band, AC/DC. The first section has a sparse, open feel and is centered around the *A major* (Fig. 1) and *A minor* (Fig. 2) blues scales. Both scales work equally well, the second section is centered more around E. For this part you can use either E minor pentatonic (Fig. 3) or G major pentatonic (Fig. 4), since both of these scales are made up of the same notes, this makes them modes of each other. For the third section, you can also use both Fig. 3 and Fig. 4.

The first sample lick (Fig. 5) is designed to work over the first section and begins by bending the note D on the G string up a whole step to E. You must pick this string eight more times while keeping it bent. The eighth time you will release the bend and continue the phrase as written. The next lick (Fig. 6) works over the second section. When performing this phrase, slide into the first note from only one or two frets below it (i.e. 12th or 13th fret). The last lick (Fig. 7) works against the third section and begins by bending the 14th fret of the G string up a whole step and holding the bend while you play other notes on the high E and B strings. This type of bend gives the lick a country flavor. This technique is repeated again at the end of the lick. Make sure that you keep the bent note ringing and in tune while you are playing the other notes after it.

*Key signature denotes A Mixolydian

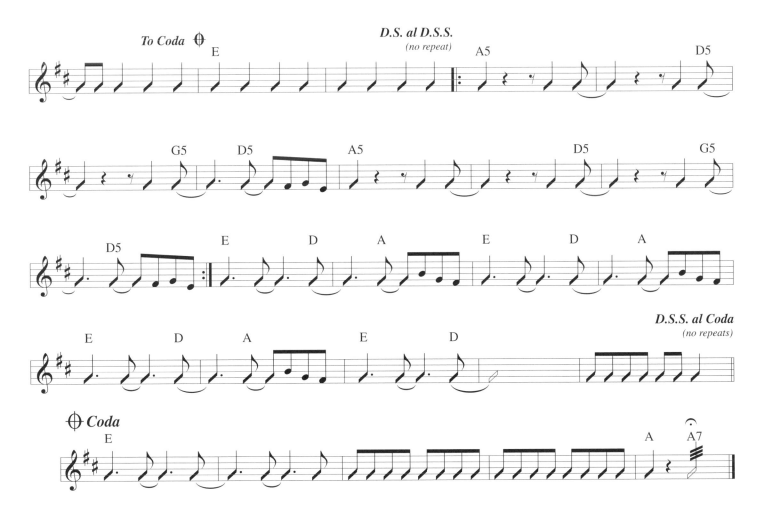

Scales for "Young Agnes"

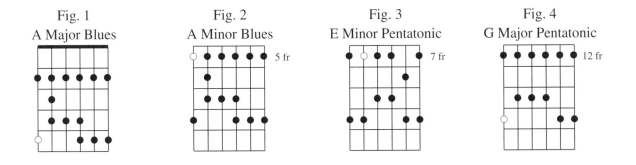

Fig. 1	Fig. 2	Fig. 3	Fig. 4
A Major Blues	A Minor Blues	E Minor Pentatonic	G Major Pentatonic

Sample Licks for "Young Agnes"

Fig. 5

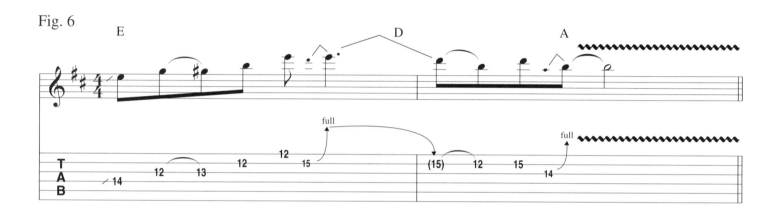

Fig. 6

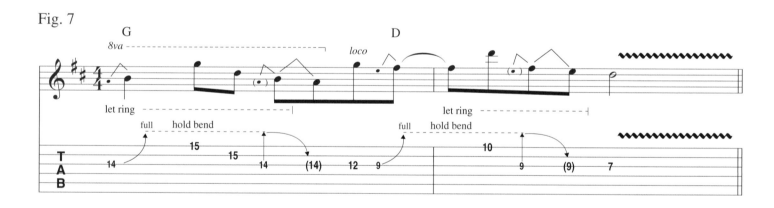

Fig. 7

HOT AND COLD

This tune has a slow funky feel and is centered around G. Over the verse and chorus sections, you can improvise with the *G minor blues* scales found in Figures 1 and 2. When you get to the bridge, try using *D minor blues* (Fig. 3) or *D Mixolydian* (Fig. 4). Remember again that you can move any scale fingering twelve frets up or down from where it's written and it will still work.

All three sample phrases are written to work over the verse section of the chart. The first phrase (Fig. 5) begins with an ascending *G minor pentatonic* scale. Make sure you only bend the Bb at the end of the phrase up a half step and not a whole step. The next lick (Fig. 6) involves bending the G string up a whole step and keeping it bent and ringing while you play other notes on the E and B strings. The final phrase (Fig. 7) incorporates a descending four-note sequence, or pattern, from the G minor pentatonic scale. Be sure to follow the articulation markings that are written for this lick. They will help you play this phrase with greater ease.

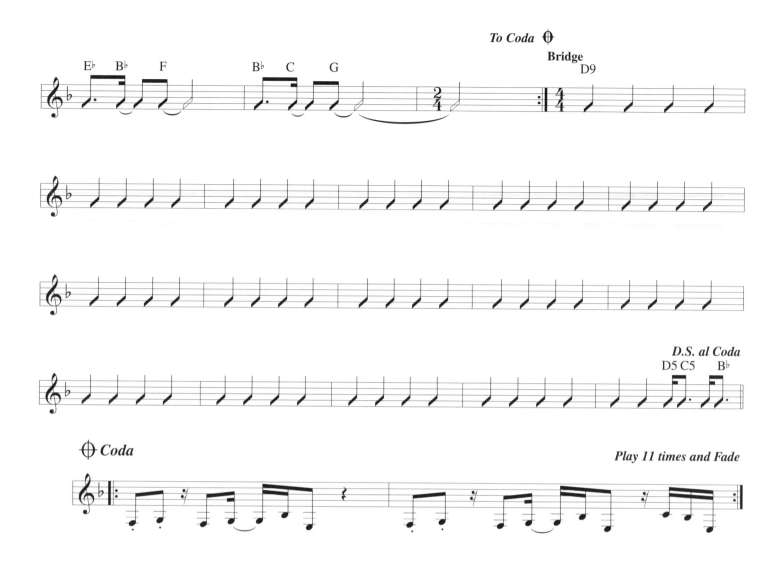

Scales for "Hot and Cold"

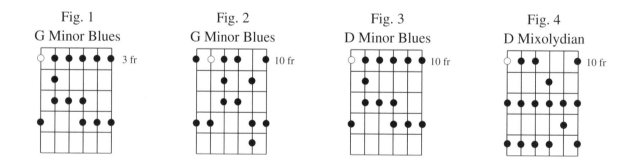

Fig. 1
G Minor Blues

Fig. 2
G Minor Blues

Fig. 3
D Minor Blues

Fig. 4
D Mixolydian

Sample Licks for "Hot and Cold"

Fig. 5

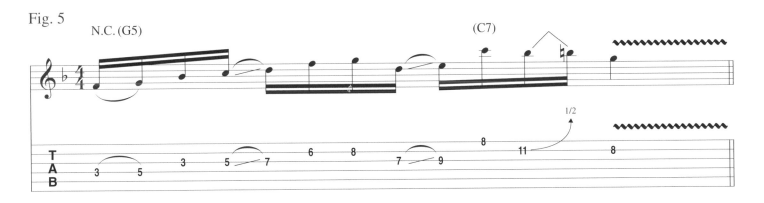

Fig. 6

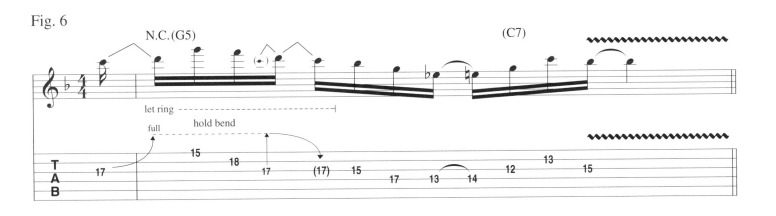

Fig. 7

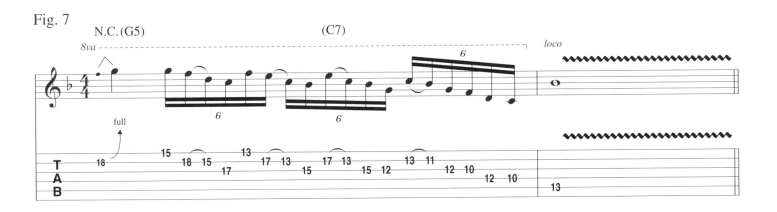

NERVOSA

This tune is inspired by the group Nirvana and employs a rhythmic groove found in many of their songs. There are two basic tonalities used in this exercise: C minor and F minor. The chorus, verse and interlude are in C minor and the bridge is in F minor. Use *C minor pentatonic* (Fig. 1) and *C Aeolian* (Fig. 2) to improvise against the chorus, verse, and interlude, and use *F minor pentatonic* (Fig. 3) and *F Aeolian* (Fig. 4) over the bridge. Don't let the sparseness of the interlude throw you off while you're improvising. Playing with only a drum accompaniment can be very liberating and gives you the freedom to play almost anything!

The first lick (Fig. 5) works over the chorus or verse and starts with what some people call an "oblique" bend. This involves picking two strings simultaneously but bending only one. In this case, you are to pick the B and G strings but only bend the G string. This may take some practice, so be patient. The next phrase (Fig. 6) should be played over the bridge. It begins with a "double stop," which means you play two strings with one finger (your first finger in this case). The last phrase uses many doublestops before ending with a quick C minor pentatonic run.

Scales for "Nervosa"

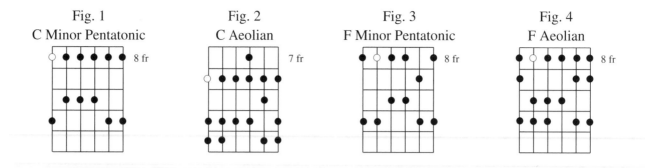

Sample Licks for "Nervosa"

Fig. 5

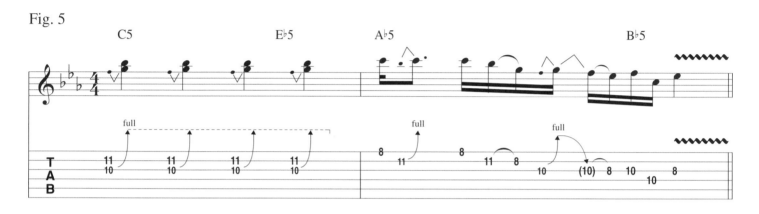

Fig. 6

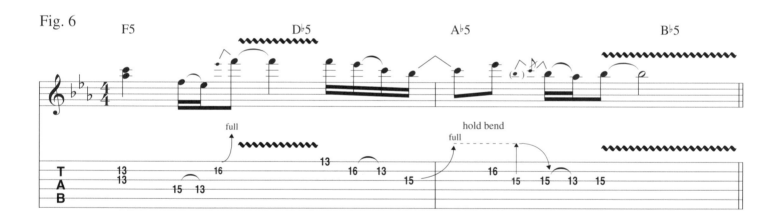

Fig. 7

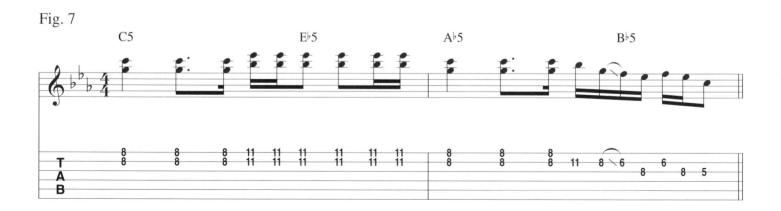

DAISY

"Daisy" is a punk-rock influenced tune in the style of the Ramones and Green Day. It's essentially made up of two sections, both of which are in the key of G major. At the end, the exercise modulates (changes keys) up a whole step to A major. To improvise over the first part (in G) use the *G major pentatonic* (Fig. 1) and the *G major scale* (Fig. 2). The "coda" is where the modulation to the key "A" occurs. For this section use *A major pentatonic* (Fig. 3) and the *A major scale* (Fig. 4).

The first lick in Fig. 5 is typical of many punk-rock solos. The first three measures each contain a repeating eighth-note pattern that follows the chords written above. The next lick (Fig. 6) also begins with a standard punk-guitar riff. In the first measure of Fig. 5, make sure that you only hear the bend go "up," not "up and down." The last phrase (Fig. 7) is a melodic single-note idea that clearly outlines the chords. If you're soloing with just a bass and drum accompaniment, then outlining the chords is a good way to clarify the harmony without actually playing chords.

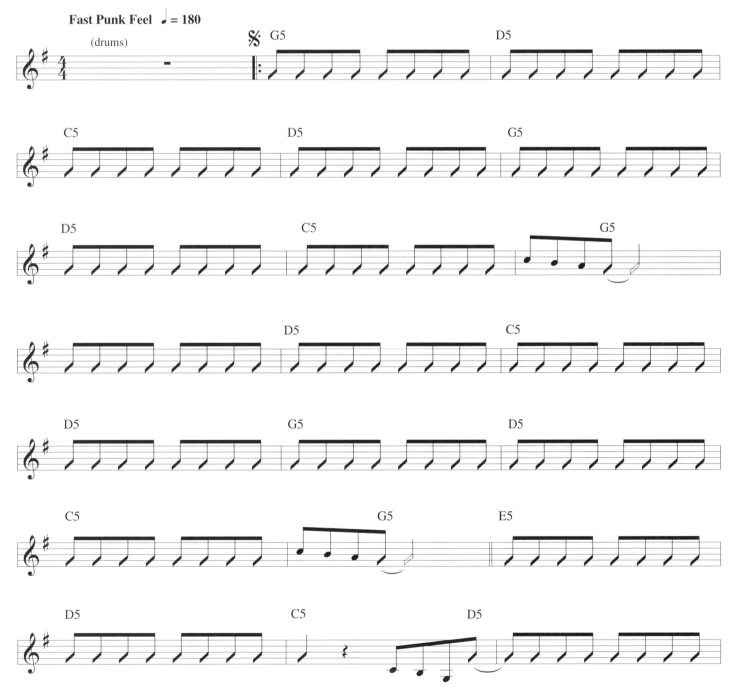

Daisy

Scales for "Daisy"

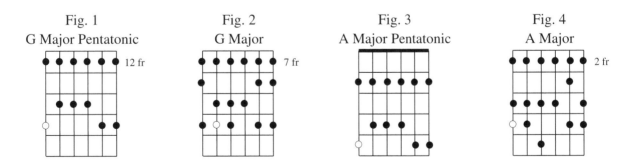

Fig. 1	Fig. 2	Fig. 3	Fig. 4
G Major Pentatonic	G Major	A Major Pentatonic	A Major

Sample Licks for "Daisy"

Fig. 5

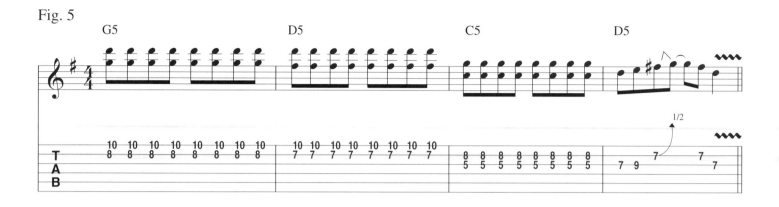

Fig. 6

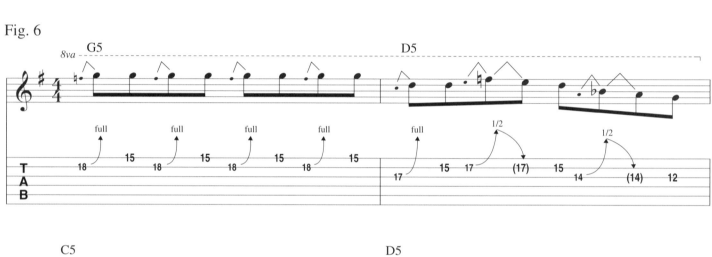

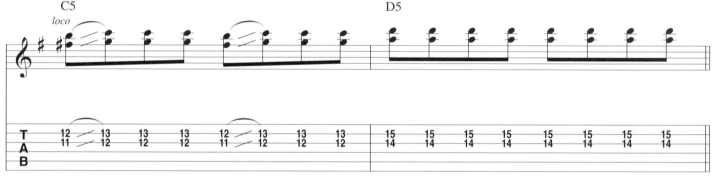

Fig. 7

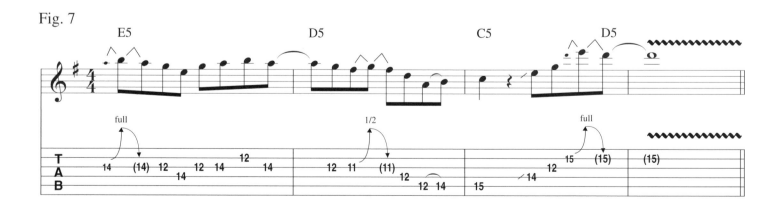

Daisy

GOOD COMPANY

This tune has a medium rock-shuffle feel and is based around the *F♯ minor blues* scale. Over the verse and chorus, you can improvise with the *F♯ minor blues* scale in Fig. 1 or the *A major pentatonic* scale in Fig. 4. Things get a little more complex over the bridge. For the first and fifth measures of the bridge, use *G major pentatonic* (Fig. 2); for the second and sixth measures, use *D major pentatonic* (Fig. 3). Over the third and seventh bars, use *A major pentatonic* (Fig. 4) and over the fourth and eighth measures, use *E major pentatonic* (Fig. 5). For the ninth and last measure of the bridge, go back to *F♯ minor blues* (Fig. 1).

The first lick (Fig. 6) contains a pre-bend, or "ghost bend," during the second half of the second beat in measure 1. A pre-bend is done by picking a string after you've bent it, but not before. In the next lick (Fig. 7), be sure to make the first bend a half step, the second bend a whole step, and the third bend a half step. The last phrase (Fig. 8) works over the bridge. Keep both bends ringing and in tune while you play the notes that follow them.

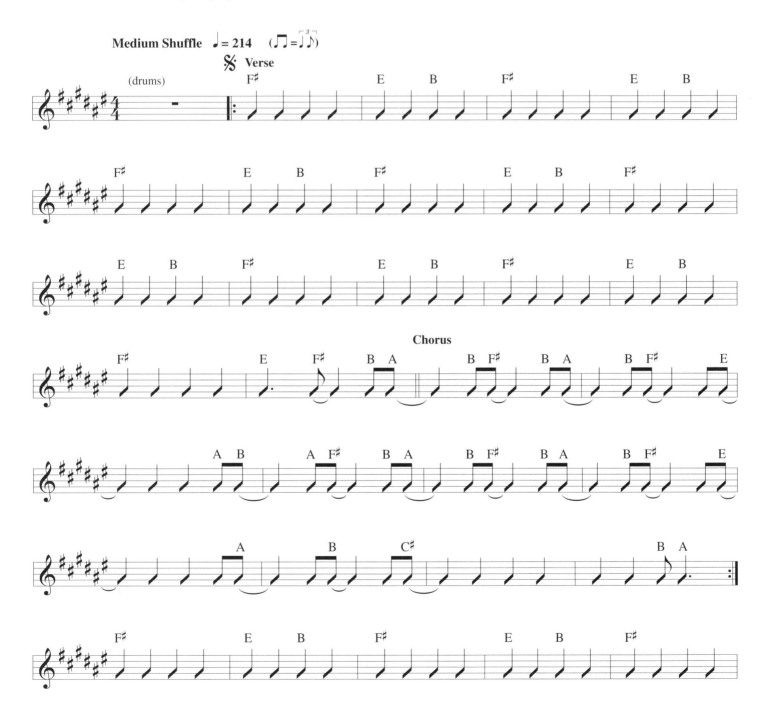

Good Company

Scales for "Good Company"

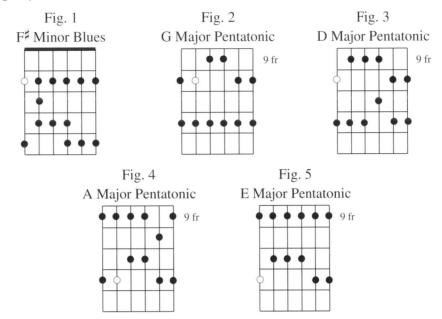

Fig. 1
F# Minor Blues

Fig. 2
G Major Pentatonic

Fig. 3
D Major Pentatonic

Fig. 4
A Major Pentatonic

Fig. 5
E Major Pentatonic

Sample Licks for "Good Company"

Fig. 6

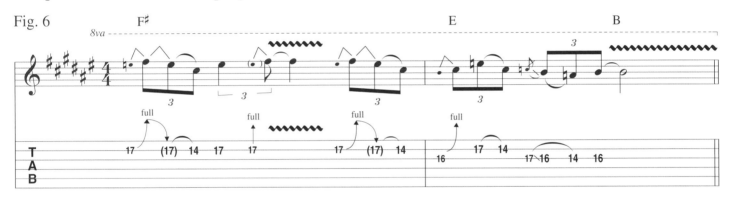

Fig. 7

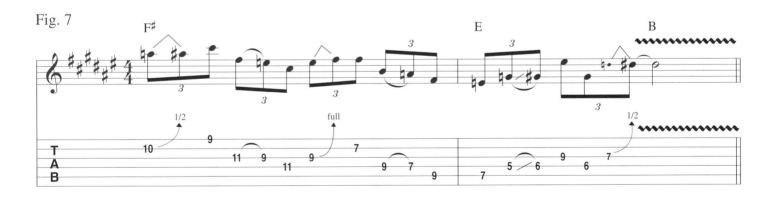

Fig. 8

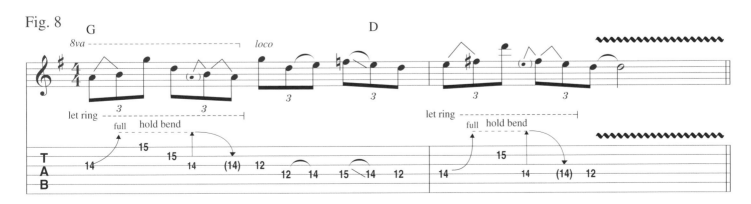

ALL HAIL SAMMY

Most of this tune is based around the key of A minor or its relative major, C. You can use any of the sample scales in Figs 1-4 to improvise over the verse or bridge sections. For the chorus, use only Figs. 1 and 2 (*A minor blues* and *A minor pentatonic,* respectively). This exercise has a comfortable tempo and feel and should give you plenty of room to improvise at whatever pace you choose.

The first lick (Fig. 5) works over the verse, clearly outlining each chord. It's important that the two bends in the first measure are not audibly released. You should only hear the pitchs go "up," not "up and down." The next phrase (Fig. 6) works against the chorus and contains a "tapped" note on the second beat of the second measure. (To tap this note, simply "hammer" the 20th fret of the high E string with any finger of your picking hand.) The last phrase (Fig. 7) begins by bending the 15th fret of the B string up a whole step and holding it while you play the 15th fret of the high E string. Make sure that the second bend in the first measure is only a quarter step and not a half or whole step. (A quarter-step bend is a very small bend that makes a note sound slightly out of tune.)

All Hail Sammy

Scales for "All Hail Sammy"

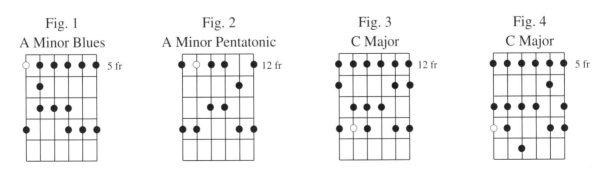

Fig. 1
A Minor Blues

Fig. 2
A Minor Pentatonic

Fig. 3
C Major

Fig. 4
C Major

Sample Licks for "All Hail Sammy"

Fig. 5

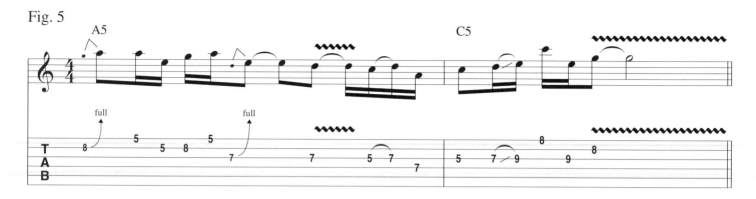

Fig. 6

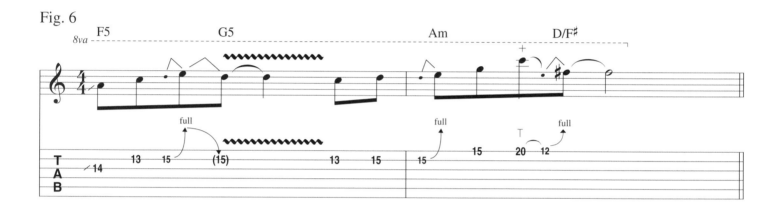

Fig. 7

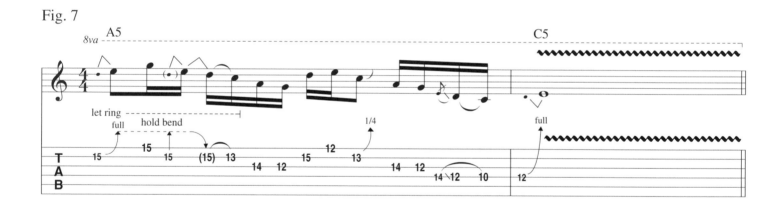

CRAWLING ALONG

"Crawling Along," the slowest of all the tunes in this chapter, is tonally centered around E minor. There are several scale choices for improvising over this progression. *E minor pentatonic* (Fig. 1) can be used universally over the entire tune. *E Dorian* (Fig. 2) works well against the A/C♯ chord in the verse and the A7 chord during the bridge. The *E Aeolian* (Fig. 3) and *B Phrygian* scale (Fig. 4) can be used over the entire chorus as well as the Em7 and Am/C chords in the verse. They can also be used to improvise over the G, C, and D chords during the bridge. The best way to start using a new scale is to pick one area of the progression that the new scale works over and just focus on using it there. This will gradually train your mind and hands to be able to switch scales in midstream.

The first phrase (Fig. 5) is comprised only of notes from the E minor pentatonic scale. Be sure to keep the second bend held up and ringing while you play the two notes that follow it. The next lick (Fig. 6) works over the chorus and incorporates finger vibrato on three different notes. Be careful not to let the second bend drop in pitch while applying vibrato. The last phrase (Fig. 7) is possibly the most difficult in this book. Make sure you let the second-to-last note of the first measure ring into the last note. Also pay close attention to the slur (hammer-on and pull-off) markings for this lick.

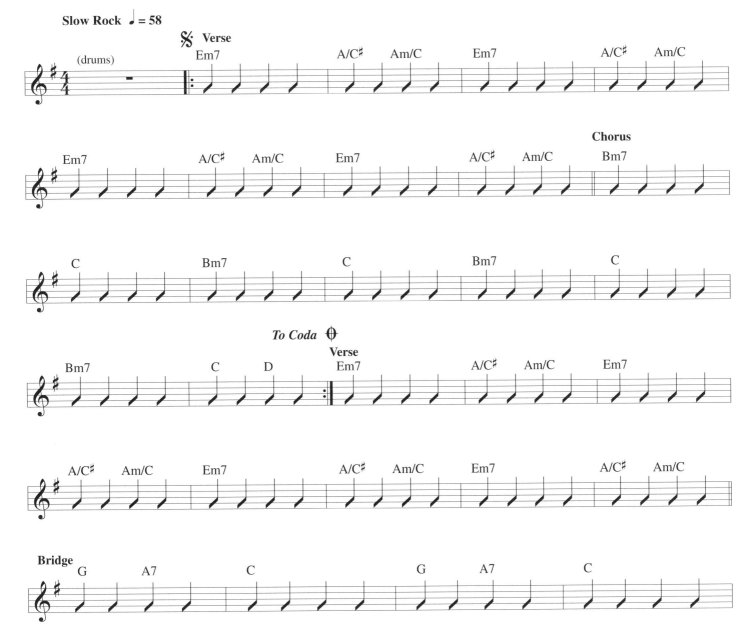

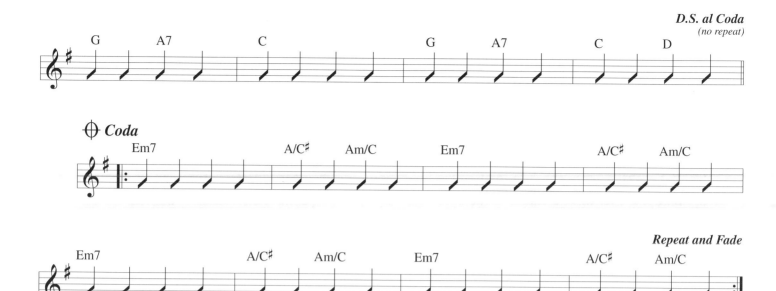

Scales for "Crawling Along"

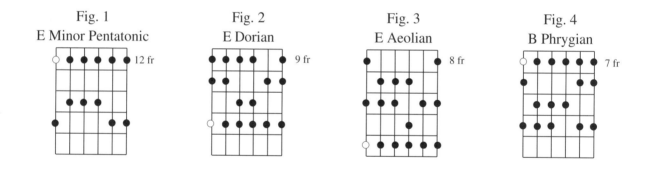

Fig. 1
E Minor Pentatonic
12 fr

Fig. 2
E Dorian
9 fr

Fig. 3
E Aeolian
8 fr

Fig. 4
B Phrygian
7 fr

Sample Licks for "Crawling Along"

Fig. 5

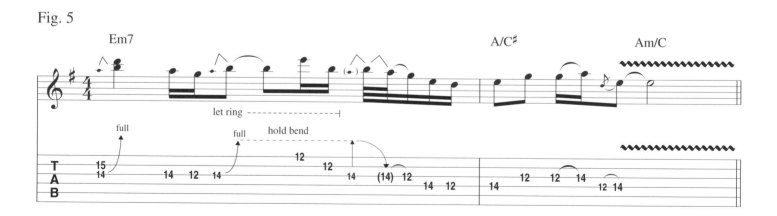

Crawling Along

Fig. 6

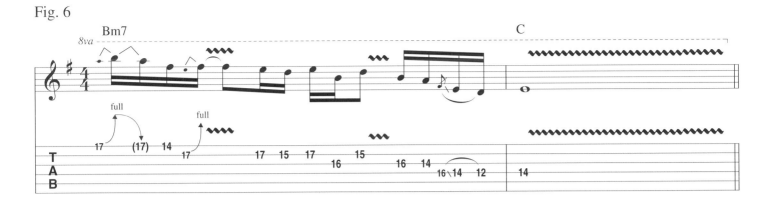

Fig. 7

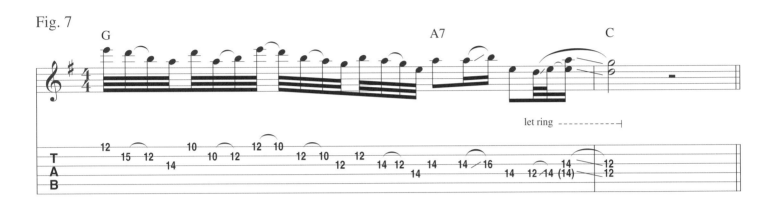

SLASH AND BURN

"Slash and Burn" has a fast, sixteenth-note funk feel, except for the bridge section, which is mostly made up of long, held chords. The main tonal center for this tune is the chord D7♯9. Use the *D minor blues* scale (Figs. 1 and 3) to improvise over the verse and chorus. For the bridge, try using *A Aeolian* (Fig. 2). (Remember that all scale fingerings will work twelve frets above or below where they're written.)

The first lick (Fig. 4) should be played over the verse or chorus and is a classic example of how to manipulate the D minor blues scale. The main challenge is in moving from one string to another with the same finger at the same fret. Try not to actually lift your finger off each string when moving, just "roll" your finger so that the tip of your finger is playing the lower string and the fleshy part (below the tip) is playing the higher string. The second phrase should be played without a strict rhythmic feel. Remember to make the second bend in this lick two whole steps wide. (You'll have to bend the string very far to do this!) The final phrase covers a large range of notes. Notice the quick slides and pull-offs in the second measure. (Make sure to execute the slides with your third finger.)

Slash and Burn

Scales for "Slash and Burn"

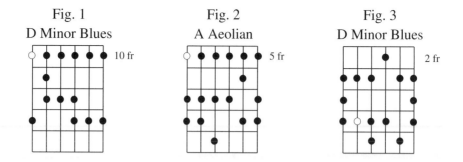

Fig. 1
D Minor Blues
10 fr

Fig. 2
A Aeolian
5 fr

Fig. 3
D Minor Blues
2 fr

Sample Licks for "Slash and Burn"

Fig. 4

Fig. 5

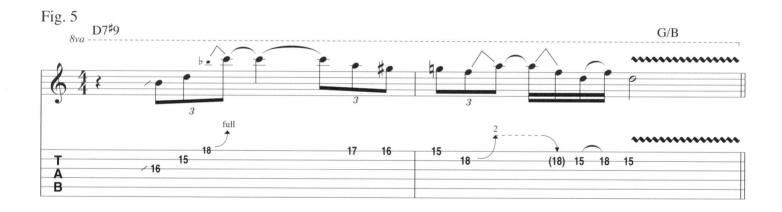

Fig. 6

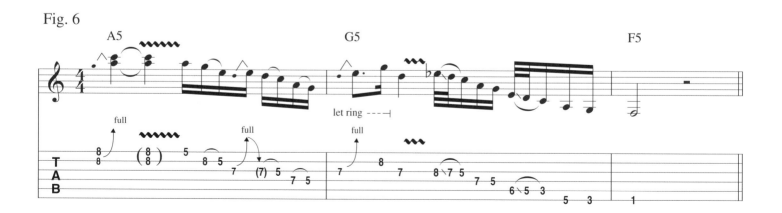

Slash and Burn

ODDS AND ENDS

The last exercise, "Odds and Ends," is an example of how odd and shifting meters can be used in a rock context. The term *meter* refers to the number of beats in each measure. A song with an odd meter has an odd number of *beats* in each measure (with the exception of three beats, which is considered a "waltz"). For this tune, we begin with the verse in 5/4 time (five beats per measure) and then "shift" to 4/4 time during the chorus and bridge. If you're not used to playing in odd meters, it may take some time before you feel comfortable soloing over this chart.

The main scales for this tune are *F♯ minor pentatonic* (Fig. 1) and *A major pentatonic* (Fig. 2). These scales are actually made up of the same notes, making them "modes" of each other. You can use Figs. 1 and 2 any time over the verse and chorus. When you get to the bridge you can continue to use Figs. 1 and 2 against the A chord, but you should switch to *C♯ minor pentatonic* (Fig. 3) over the C♯m chord. For the G and D chords, try using *D major* (Fig. 4). Over the last chord of the bridge (E), you can go back to using either Fig. 1 or Fig. 2.

The first phrase (Fig. 5) should be played during the verse. It contains a quick "reverse bend" on the last beat of the second measure. To do this, you must bend the B string up a half step without picking it, then pick the string and simultaneously yank it back to its original unbent position. The second lick (Fig. 6) works over the chorus. It begins by bending the first note (on the G string) up a half step and holding it there while you play the next note (on the B string). Make sure you catch the grace note slides at the end of the third measure. The last lick (Fig. 7) is played over the first three measures of the bridge and requires a bit of a stretch. Remember to observe all slur markings for this lick rather than trying to pick every note.

Bridge
Half-Time Feel

(drums)

D.C. al Fine
(no repeat)
Verse

1st time; continue through to Fine 2nd time

Fine
Play 6 Times and Fade

Scales for "Odds and Ends"

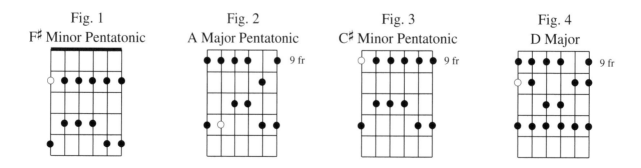

Fig. 1	Fig. 2	Fig. 3	Fig. 4
F# Minor Pentatonic	A Major Pentatonic	C# Minor Pentatonic	D Major

Sample Licks for "Odds and Ends"

Fig. 5

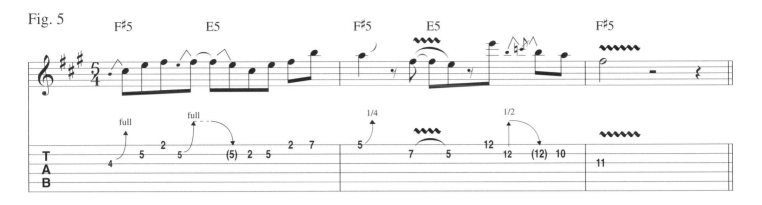

Fig. 6

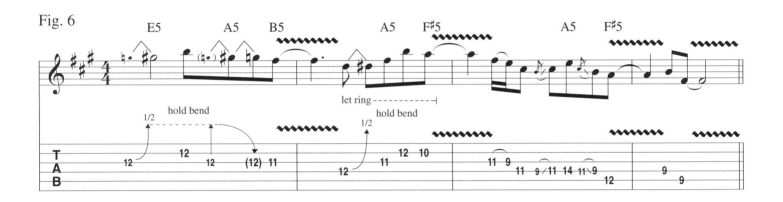

Fig. 7

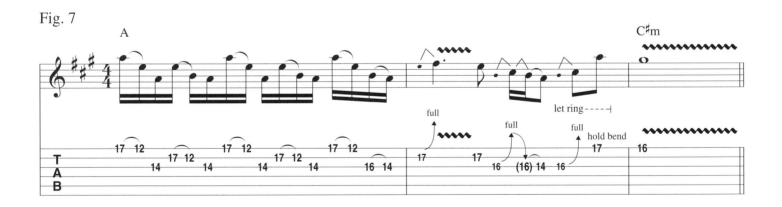

Guitar Notation Legend

Guitar Music can be notated three different ways: on a *musical staff*, in *tablature*, and in *rhythm slashes*.

RHYTHM SLASHES are written above the staff. Strum chords in the rhythm indicated. Use the chord diagrams found at the top of the first page of the transcription for the appropriate chord voicings. Round noteheads indicate single notes.

THE MUSICAL STAFF shows pitches and rhythms and is divided by bar lines into measures. Pitches are named after the first seven letters of the alphabet.

TABLATURE graphically represents the guitar fingerboard. Each horizontal line represents a a string, and each number represents a fret.

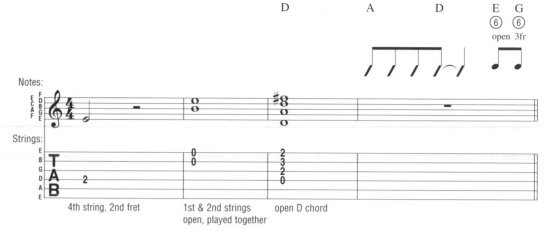

4th string, 2nd fret

1st & 2nd strings open, played together

open D chord

Definitions for Special Guitar Notation

HALF-STEP BEND: Strike the note and bend up 1/2 step.

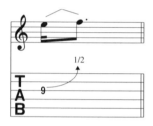

WHOLE-STEP BEND: Strike the note and bend up one step.

GRACE NOTE BEND: Strike the note and bend up as indicated. The first note does not take up any time.

SLIGHT (MICROTONE) BEND: Strike the note and bend up 1/4 step.

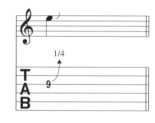

BEND AND RELEASE: Strike the note and bend up as indicated, then release back to the original note. Only the first note is struck.

PRE-BEND: Bend the note as indicated, then strike it.

PRE-BEND AND RELEASE: Bend the note as indicated. Strike it and release the bend back to the original note.

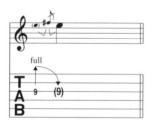

UNISON BEND: Strike the two notes simultaneously and bend the lower note up to the pitch of the higher.

VIBRATO: The string is vibrated by rapidly bending and releasing the note with the fretting hand.

WIDE VIBRATO: The pitch is varied to a greater degree by vibrating with the fretting hand.

HAMMER-ON: Strike the first (lower) note with one finger, then sound the higher note (on the same string) with another finger by fretting it without picking.

PULL-OFF: Place both fingers on the notes to be sounded. Strike the first note and without picking, pull the finger off to sound the second (lower) note.

LEGATO SLIDE: Strike the first note and then slide the same fret-hand finger up or down to the second note. The second note is not struck.

SHIFT SLIDE: Same as legato slide, except the second note is struck.

TRILL: Very rapidly alternate between the notes indicated by continuously hammering on and pulling off.

TAPPING: Hammer ("tap") the fret indicated with the pick-hand index or middle finger and pull off to the note fretted by the fret hand.

NATURAL HARMONIC: Strike the note while the fret-hand lightly touches the string directly over the fret indicated.

PINCH HARMONIC: The note is fretted normally and a harmonic is produced by adding the edge of the thumb or the tip of the index finger of the pick hand to the normal pick attack.

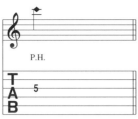

HARP HARMONIC: The note is fretted normally and a harmonic is produced by gently resting the pick hand's index finger directly above the indicated fret (in parentheses) while the pick hand's thumb or pick assists by plucking the appropriate string.

PICK SCRAPE: The edge of the pick is rubbed down (or up) the string, producing a scratchy sound.

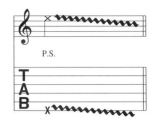

MUFFLED STRINGS: A percussive sound is produced by laying the fret hand across the string(s) without depressing, and striking them with the pick hand.

PALM MUTING: The note is partially muted by the pick hand lightly touching the string(s) just before the bridge.

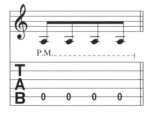

RAKE: Drag the pick across the strings indicated with a single motion.

TREMOLO PICKING: The note is picked as rapidly and continuously as possible.

ARPEGGIATE: Play the notes of the chord indicated by quickly rolling them from bottom to top.

VIBRATO BAR DIVE AND RETURN: The pitch of the note or chord is dropped a specified number of steps (in rhythm) then returned to the original pitch.

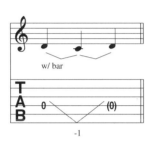

VIBRATO BAR SCOOP: Depress the bar just before striking the note, then quickly release the bar.

VIBRATO BAR DIP: Strike the note and then immediately drop a specified number of steps, then release back to the original pitch.

Additional Musical Definitions

 (accent) • Accentuate note (play it louder)

 (accent) • Accentuate note with great intensity

 (staccato) • Play the note short

 • Downstroke

∨ • Upstroke

D.S. al Coda • Go back to the sign (𝄋), then play until the measure marked "*To Coda*," then skip to the section labelled "*Coda*."

D.S. al Fine • Go back to the beginning of the song and play until the measure marked "*Fine*" (end).

Rhy. Fig. • Label used to recall a recurring accompaniment pattern (usually chordal).

Riff • Label used to recall composed, melodic lines (usually single notes) which recur.

Fill • Label used to identify a brief melodic figure which is to be inserted into the arrangement.

Rhy. Fill • A chordal version of a Fill.

tacet • Instrument is silent (drops out).

 • Repeat measures between signs.

 • When a repeated section has different endings, play the first ending only the first time and the second ending only the second time.

NOTE: Tablature numbers in parentheses mean:
1. The note is being sustained over a system (note in standard notation is tied), or
2. The note is sustained, but a new articulation (such as a hammer-on, pull-off, slide or vibrato begins, or
3. The note is a barely audible "ghost" note (note in standard notation is also in parentheses).

HAL•LEONARD GUITAR PLAY•ALONG

This series will help you play your favorite songs quickly and easily. Just follow the tab **INCLUDES TAB** and listen to the CD to the hear how the guitar should sound, and then play along using the separate backing tracks. Mac or PC users can also slow down the tempo without changing pitch by using the CD in their computer. The melody and lyrics are included in the book so that you can sing or simply follow along.

VOL. 1 – ROCK	00699570 / $16.99
VOL. 2 – ACOUSTIC	00699569 / $16.95
VOL. 3 – HARD ROCK	00699573 / $16.95
VOL. 4 – POP/ROCK	00699571 / $16.99
VOL. 5 – MODERN ROCK	00699574 / $16.99
VOL. 6 – '90S ROCK	00699572 / $16.99
VOL. 7 – BLUES	00699575 / $16.95
VOL. 8 – ROCK	00699585 / $14.99
VOL. 9 – PUNK ROCK	00699576 / $14.95
VOL. 10 – ACOUSTIC	00699586 / $16.95
VOL. 11 – EARLY ROCK	00699579 / $14.95
VOL. 12 – POP/ROCK	00699587 / $14.95
VOL. 13 – FOLK ROCK	00699581 / $15.99
VOL. 14 – BLUES ROCK	00699582 / $16.95
VOL. 15 – R&B	00699583 / $14.95
VOL. 16 – JAZZ	00699584 / $15.95
VOL. 17 – COUNTRY	00699588 / $15.95
VOL. 18 – ACOUSTIC ROCK	00699577 / $15.95
VOL. 19 – SOUL	00699578 / $14.99
VOL. 20 – ROCKABILLY	00699580 / $14.95
VOL. 21 – YULETIDE	00699602 / $14.95
VOL. 22 – CHRISTMAS	00699600 / $15.95
VOL. 23 – SURF	00699635 / $14.95
VOL. 24 – ERIC CLAPTON	00699649 / $17.99
VOL. 25 – LENNON & MCCARTNEY	00699642 / $16.99
VOL. 26 – ELVIS PRESLEY	00699643 / $14.95
VOL. 27 – DAVID LEE ROTH	00699645 / $16.95
VOL. 28 – GREG KOCH	00699646 / $14.95
VOL. 29 – BOB SEGER	00699647 / $15.99
VOL. 30 – KISS	00699644 / $16.99
VOL. 31 – CHRISTMAS HITS	00699652 / $14.95
VOL. 32 – THE OFFSPRING	00699653 / $14.95
VOL. 33 – ACOUSTIC CLASSICS	00699656 / $16.95
VOL. 34 – CLASSIC ROCK	00699658 / $16.95
VOL. 35 – HAIR METAL	00699660 / $16.95
VOL. 36 – SOUTHERN ROCK	00699661 / $16.95
VOL. 37 – ACOUSTIC METAL	00699662 / $16.95
VOL. 38 – BLUES	00699663 / $16.95
VOL. 39 – '80S METAL	00699664 / $16.99
VOL. 40 – INCUBUS	00699668 / $17.95
VOL. 41 – ERIC CLAPTON	00699669 / $16.95
VOL. 42 – 2000S ROCK	00699670 / $16.99
VOL. 43 – LYNYRD SKYNYRD	00699681 / $17.95
VOL. 44 – JAZZ	00699689 / $14.99
VOL. 45 – TV THEMES	00699718 / $14.95
VOL. 46 – MAINSTREAM ROCK	00699722 / $16.95
VOL. 47 – HENDRIX SMASH HITS	00699723 / $19.95
VOL. 48 – AEROSMITH CLASSICS	00699724 / $17.99
VOL. 49 – STEVIE RAY VAUGHAN	00699725 / $17.99
VOL. 51 – ALTERNATIVE '90S	00699727 / $14.99
VOL. 52 – FUNK	00699728 / $14.95
VOL. 53 – DISCO	00699729 / $14.99
VOL. 54 – HEAVY METAL	00699730 / $14.95
VOL. 55 – POP METAL	00699731 / $14.95

VOL. 56 – FOO FIGHTERS	00699749 / $15.99
VOL. 57 – SYSTEM OF A DOWN	00699751 / $14.95
VOL. 58 – BLINK-182	00699772 / $14.95
VOL. 59 – CHET ATKINS	00702347 / $16.99
VOL. 60 – 3 DOORS DOWN	00699774 / $14.95
VOL. 61 – SLIPKNOT	00699775 / $16.99
VOL. 62 – CHRISTMAS CAROLS	00699798 / $12.95
VOL. 63 – CREEDENCE CLEARWATER REVIVAL	00699802 / $16.99
VOL. 64 – THE ULTIMATE OZZY OSBOURNE	00699803 / $16.99
VOL. 65 – THE DOORS	00699806 / $16.99
VOL. 66 – THE ROLLING STONES	00699807 / $16.95
VOL. 67 – BLACK SABBATH	00699808 / $16.99
VOL. 68 – PINK FLOYD – DARK SIDE OF THE MOON	00699809 / $16.99
VOL. 69 – ACOUSTIC FAVORITES	00699810 / $14.95
VOL. 70 – OZZY OSBOURNE	00699805 / $16.99
VOL. 71 – CHRISTIAN ROCK	00699824 / $14.95
VOL. 72 – ACOUSTIC '90S	00699827 / $14.95
VOL. 73 – BLUESY ROCK	00699829 / $16.99
VOL. 74 – PAUL BALOCHE	00699831 / $14.95
VOL. 75 – TOM PETTY	00699882 / $16.99
VOL. 76 – COUNTRY HITS	00699884 / $14.95
VOL. 77 – BLUEGRASS	00699910 / $14.99
VOL. 78 – NIRVANA	00700132 / $16.99
VOL. 79 – NEIL YOUNG	00700133 / $24.99
VOL. 80 – ACOUSTIC ANTHOLOGY	00700175 / $19.95
VOL. 81 – ROCK ANTHOLOGY	00700176 / $22.99
VOL. 82 – EASY SONGS	00700177 / $12.99
VOL. 83 – THREE CHORD SONGS	00700178 / $16.99
VOL. 84 – STEELY DAN	00700200 / $16.99
VOL. 85 – THE POLICE	00700269 / $16.99
VOL. 86 – BOSTON	00700465 / $16.99
VOL. 87 – ACOUSTIC WOMEN	00700763 / $14.99
VOL. 88 – GRUNGE	00700467 / $16.99
VOL. 90 – CLASSICAL POP	00700469 / $14.99
VOL. 91 – BLUES INSTRUMENTALS	00700505 / $14.99
VOL. 92 – EARLY ROCK INSTRUMENTALS	00700506 / $14.99
VOL. 93 – ROCK INSTRUMENTALS	00700507 / $16.99
VOL. 95 – BLUES CLASSICS	00700509 / $14.99
VOL. 96 – THIRD DAY	00700560 / $14.95
VOL. 97 – ROCK BAND	00700703 / $14.99
VOL. 98 – ROCK BAND	00700704 / $14.95
VOL. 99 – ZZ TOP	00700762 / $16.99
VOL. 100 – B.B. KING	00700466 / $16.99
VOL. 101 – SONGS FOR BEGINNERS	00701917 / $14.99
VOL. 102 – CLASSIC PUNK	00700769 / $14.99
VOL. 103 – SWITCHFOOT	00700773 / $16.99
VOL. 104 – DUANE ALLMAN	00700846 / $16.99
VOL. 106 – WEEZER	00700958 / $14.99
VOL. 107 – CREAM	00701069 / $16.99
VOL. 108 – THE WHO	00701053 / $16.99

VOL. 109 – STEVE MILLER	00701054 / $14.99
VOL. 111 – JOHN MELLENCAMP	00701056 / $14.99
VOL. 112 – QUEEN	00701052 / $16.99
VOL. 113 – JIM CROCE	00701058 / $15.99
VOL. 114 – BON JOVI	00701060 / $14.99
VOL. 115 – JOHNNY CASH	00701070 / $16.99
VOL. 116 – THE VENTURES	00701124 / $14.99
VOL. 118 – ERIC JOHNSON	00701353 / $14.99
VOL. 119 – AC/DC CLASSICS	00701356 / $17.99
VOL. 120 – PROGRESSIVE ROCK	00701457 / $14.99
VOL. 121 – U2	00701508 / $16.99
VOL. 123 – LENNON & MCCARTNEY ACOUSTIC	00701614 / $16.99
VOL. 124 – MODERN WORSHIP	00701629 / $14.99
VOL. 125 – JEFF BECK	00701687 / $16.99
VOL. 126 – BOB MARLEY	00701701 / $16.99
VOL. 127 – 1970S ROCK	00701739 / $14.99
VOL. 128 – 1960S ROCK	00701740 / $14.99
VOL. 129 – MEGADETH	00701741 / $16.99
VOL. 131 – 1990S ROCK	00701743 / $14.99
VOL. 132 – COUNTRY ROCK	00701757 / $15.99
VOL. 133 – TAYLOR SWIFT	00701894 / $16.99
VOL. 134 – AVENGED SEVENFOLD	00701906 / $16.99
VOL. 136 – GUITAR THEMES	00701922 / $14.99
VOL. 138 – BLUEGRASS CLASSICS	00701967 / $14.99
VOL. 139 – GARY MOORE	00702370 / $16.99
VOL. 140 – MORE STEVIE RAY VAUGHAN	00702396 / $17.99
VOL. 141 – ACOUSTIC HITS	00702401 / $16.99
VOL. 142 – KINGS OF LEON	00702418 / $16.99
VOL. 144 – DJANGO REINHARDT	00702531 / $16.99
VOL. 145 – DEF LEPPARD	00702532 / $16.99
VOL. 147 – SIMON & GARFUNKEL	14041591 / $16.99
VOL. 149 – AC/DC HITS	14041593 / $17.99
VOL. 150 – ZAKK WYLDE	02501717 / $16.99
VOL. 153 – RED HOT CHILI PEPPERS	00702990 / $19.99
VOL. 157 – FLEETWOOD MAC	00101382 / $16.99
VOL. 158 – ULTIMATE CHRISTMAS	00101889 / $14.99
VOL. 161 – THE EAGLES – ACOUSTIC	00102659 / $17.99
VOL. 162 – THE EAGLES HITS	00102667 / $17.99
VOL. 163 – PANTERA	00103036 / $16.99
VOL. 166 – MODERN BLUES	00700764 / $16.99
VOL. 168 – KISS	00113421 / $16.99
VOL. 169 – TAYLOR SWIFT	00115982 / $16.99
VOL. 170 – THREE DAYS GRACE	00117337 / $16.99

Complete song lists available online.

Prices, contents, and availability subject to change without notice.

HAL•LEONARD®
CORPORATION
7777 W. BLUEMOUND RD. P.O. BOX 13819 MILWAUKEE, WI 53213
www.halleonard.com

0713